The Breakdown of Austin Rover

A Case-Study in the Failure of Business Strategy and Industrial Policy

Karel Williams
John Williams
Colin Haslam

BERG
Leamington Spa / Hamburg / New York
Distributed exclusively in the US and Canada by
St. Martin's Press New York

First published in 1987 by
Berg Publishers Limited
24 Binswood Avenue, Leamington Spa, CV32 5SQ, UK
Schenefelder Landstr. 14K, 2000 Hamburg 55, West Germany
Room 400, 175 Fifth Avenue, New York, NY 10010, USA

British Library Cataloguing in Publication Data

Williams, Karel
The breakdown of Austin Rover: a case-study in the failure of business strategy and industrial policy.
1. British Leyland Motor Corporation—History
I. Title II. Williams, L. J. III. Haslam, Colin
338.7′629224′0941 HD9710.G74B65

ISBN 0–85496–515–7
ISBN 0–85496–516–5 Pbk

Library of Congress Cataloging-in-Publication-Data

Wiliiams, Karel.
The breakdown of Austin Rover.

Bibliography: p.
Includes index.
1. Austin Rover Group. 2. Automobile industry and trade—Great Britain. I. Williams, John (John L.)
II. Haslam, Colin. III. Title.
HD9710.G74A868 1987 338.7′6292222 86–24449
ISBN 0–85496–515–7
ISBN 0–85496–516–5 (pbk.)

Printed in Great Britain by Billings of Worcester

Contents

1. 'The Truth About Austin Rover' 1

2. The Labour Problem? 14

3. Investment Strategy 35
  Investment in New Technology: the Justification 44
  The New Technology: Possibilities and Limitations 50
  Flexibility for What? 56

4. Market-Led Failure 67

5. No End of a Lesson 97
  What is to be Done? 107

Appendices
  Accounting for Austin Rover 118
  Production and Market Statistics 125

Select Bibliography 144

Index 147

About the Authors 150

List of Tables

1.1 Austin Rover production, home sales and exports, 1978–85 9
2.1 Man hours lost through strikes at BL 18
2.2 Comparison of European productivity in three processes 20
2.3 Volume car labour productivity at Austin Morris and Austin Rover, 1969–85 23
2.4 Breakdown of costs of producing two medium-sized saloon cars in UK factories, 1975 29
3.1 Fixed assets per man, 1972 35
3.2 Production volumes of European, American and Japanese car firms, 1984 39
3.3 Model volume at Austin Rover 39
3.4 Production volumes of the ten European best-selling cars, 1984 40
3.5 Gross assets per man employed in Austin Rover, Ford UK and BMW, 1984 41
3.6 Gross assets employed per unit of output at BL 42
3.7 Number of men replaced by one robot 45
3.8 A comparison of direct manpower in traditional and automated body building 45
3.9 Labour and capital inputs with different body building techniques 46
3.10 Machine cycle times on the Metro body line 47
3.11 Breakdown of cost of a robot assembly system 52
3.12 Nissan and VW model ranges 59
4.1 Sales of the four best-selling European motor cars in the major national markets, 1984 68
4.2 Austin Rover production, home sales and exports, 1978–85 69
4.3 Austin Rover's share of the company car market 74
4.4 Major company shares of UK new car registrations, 1979–85 76
4.5 Directly competing models from the three majors 76
4.6 Market shares of the ten best-selling cars in the UK, 1985 77

4.7 Share of the British car market claimed by Austin Rover, Ford and Vauxhall's three best-selling models 79
4.8 BL car exports, 1970–85 83
4.9 BL car exports to the EEC, 1976–83 84
4.10 BL car exports to the EEC, by country, 1976–83 85
4.11 Production volumes at Austin Rover, 1982–4 92
4.12 BL models in the top ten sales positions, 1972–85 95
5.1 Import penetration, export performance and crude trade balance, by SIC class, 1978–83 106
A.1 Austin Rover Group financial performance, 1977–84 120
A.2 Cars division: loans and fixed assets, 1977–84 123
B.1 Company shares of UK new car market 125
B.2 British Leyland production, exports and share of new car registrations, 1970–85 126
B.3 Austin Morris/Austin Rover production, exports and share of new car registrations, 1970–85 127
B.4 Fragmentation of sales in major UK market classes 128
B.5 Top ten best-selling cars in the UK, 1967–85 132
B.6 Europe's top ten models, 1984 136
B.7 Production volumes of major European, American and Japanese car producers 138
B.8 Market share held by the three best-selling models from the three major UK companies 140
B.9 BL car exports to the EEC and USA, 1976–84 142
B.10 Change in BL exports to the EEC, 1977–84 143

List of Figures

3.1 Maestro/Montego line layout 64
3.1 Sierra line layout 65

1/The Truth about Austin Rover

In July 1986 the entire enterprise of British Leyland (BL) was, at the instigation of Graham Day, its recently appointed Chairman, given a new name: the Rover Group. It is easy to see, therefore, the possibility of confusion arising between Rover Group and the object of the present study, the Austin Rover Group. Thus it should be emphasised at the outset that the term 'Austin Rover' in this book refers simply to the volume cars division. Since volume car production did not end with BL's change of name it seemed likely to be less confusing to the reader if we continued to use the term 'Austin Rover' to refer to the continuing activity and prospects of the company in car production.

Austin Rover Group was the volume car division of BL plc, the state-owned motor-car firm which also produced trucks, buses, vans and 4 × 4s. The division built Austin and Rover cars in two major assembly plants at Longbridge and Cowley which were fed with components from satellite factories such as the plant at Swindon which produces pressings. The division was a relatively recent creation; the corporate reorganisation which created the division in the early 1980s was initiated by Michael Edwardes, who became chairman of BL in late 1977. If Austin Rover represented a new organisational beginning, it is also true that the volume car business which it inherited had long been a problem. The history of this business since the early 1950s has been one of enterprise failure which is signalled by profits crisis that is then followed by corporate reorganisation and a new beginning under a different management team.

After the Second World War, there were two major British-owned car producers, Austin and Morris; the Nuffield organisation (alias Morris) had lost its way by 1952, when it merged with its rival to form BMC under Austin's Len Lord and George Harriman. The financial performance of the BMC was never sparkling and within fifteen years the company was losing money. In 1968, BMC was taken over by Leyland, a truck manufacturer which had moved into cars through the purchase of the nearly bankrupt Standard Triumph company in 1961. This merger created BLMC, which consolidated all the independent British car manufacturers (Austin Morris, Jaguar, Rover and Triumph) into a new organisation which was led by Donald Stokes and John Barber. Within seven years, there was a much more acute profits crisis; BLMC lost £76 million in 1975. At this point the company was effectively nationalised as British Leyland (BL). A new business strategy was mapped out by Sir Don Ryder and a new management team under Derek Whittaker and Alex Park began to implement that strategy. Within three years it became clear that the company was facing yet another profits crisis; profits were negligible in 1977 and 1978 and the company lost £112 million in 1979. In the early stages of this crisis, Michael Edwardes was brought in as chairman in November 1977 and the senior management team was changed yet again. Michael Edwardes chose as lieutenants men like Ray Horrocks and David Andrews, who were not identified with the failed Ryder strategy.

The problems of the volume cars business which the new management inherited in 1977 had defeated the best efforts of at least three management teams (Lord and Harriman; Stokes and Barber; Ryder, Whittaker and Park) over the previous twenty-five years. The shrewdest managers in the British car industry were those in Ford UK, which was led by Terence Beckett in the 1960s and 1970s; Ford's top management team in this period considered that the problems of the Austin Morris volume car business were insoluble largely because BMC/BLMC could only claim its 40 per cent market share by making a large number of body shells in uneconomically small quantities (Connell *et al.*, 1984, chap. VII, p. 31). Over the years, BLMC and BL poached many Ford managers; Ray Horrocks and David Andrews, who took over Michael Edwardes' executive functions after 1982, had both once worked for Ford (Connell *et al.*, 1984, chap. VII, p. 31). But, significantly, no senior figure in Ford's UK or European hierarchy was ever persuaded to accept a job in the Austin Morris volume car business. Ford managers like Terence Beckett and Bill Hayden sat through successive profits crises at Austin Morris while their own company profitably claimed 25 per cent of the UK car market with three body shells and waited for the major British car producer to go out of business. The new management thus clearly took on a daunting task in accepting the challenge of turning round the volume cars business.

At the same time we do not want to personalise the issues. In our discussion in later chapters reference is sometimes made to 'Edwardes'. Given Sir Michael's dominance during his years as chairman from 1977 to 1982, it is difficult to avoid such references. But the name is simply used as a convenient shorthand for the business strategy which was initiated after Michael Edwardes became chairman in 1977. This book has been written from published sources by a team of outsiders. Without access to internal company documents such as the memos of senior managers or the minutes of board meetings, we cannot determine which managers initiated key policies or apportion responsibility for the success or failure of those policies. That, in any case, is not our purpose. In this introduction we aim to define the business strategy of 'the Edwardes era' and then briefly discuss to what extent that strategy succeeded or failed. Subsequent chapters will analyse the reasons for success and failure which have very little to do with individual personalities and much more to do with abstract considerations such as the nature of competition in the UK car market. This is a book about enterprise calculation and miscalculation, not about individual managers as heroes and villains.

There is no doubt that when Michael Edwardes became chairman of BL in 1977, the volume cars division (which later became Austin Rover Group) was in a bad way. With much justice, the new chairman criticised 'the over-optimistic Ryder plan' which 'had postulated expansion when in reality the company lacked the models, the efficient manufacturing facilities and a management determined to get to grips with over-manning and over-capacity' (Edwardes, 1983, p. 86). The new management team formulated a strategy to deal with all these problems. This strategy was not determined all at once in a few months after November 1977 because the company went through a series of agonising reappraisals which began with the adoption of a more modest corporate plan in February 1978. Reappraisals could not be avoided because financial performance continued to deteriorate for at least three years after the managerial change-over; the BL company as a whole lost a record £380 million in 1980 when losses accounted for 13.5 per cent of the sales revenue from cars and trucks (Williams *et al.*, 1983, pp. 260–1). The strategy for cars and the rest of the company was put into nearly definitive form in the 'recovery plan' (or Corporate Recovery Programme) which was presented to the government in July 1979 and voted on by the work-force in a ballot in the autumn of that year. According to Michael Edwardes, this plan proposed 'probably the most extensive restructuring of a major public company that has ever been done in such a short period of time' (Edwardes, 1983, p. 95). The aim then was to turn the company round and make it profitable by 1982 or 1983. By the spring of 1980, the company had been blown off course by a combination of recession, inflation and a strong pound. In May of that year, the Prime Minister was told that the company required an extra £1,000 million of government funding to keep it afloat in 1981 and 1982; this crisis occasioned further efforts to cut costs (Edwardes, 1983, pp. 228–9). Nevertheless, through all the twists and turns as events unfolded in unexpected ways, the fundamentals of the strategy remained much the same from early 1979 onwards.

The new strategy represented a decisive break with the earlier Ryder approach in one key respect. Ryder had projected a large expansion of car output from 'depressed' 1975 levels. In that year Austin Morris had produced just 450,000 cars and BL as a whole (including Jaguar, Rover and Triumph) 605,000 cars (Williams *et al.*, 1983, p. 256). Ryder had assumed that the BL company would make and sell 843,000 cars by 1980 and 961,000 cars by 1985 (Williams *et al.*, 1983, p. 264). After Michael Edwardes became chairman, these plans were rejected as unrealistic and the company embarked on a programme of rationalisation which involved large-scale redundancies and closure of peripheral plants. As the financial crisis worsened, the closure programme was extended and accelerated. Capacity in the BL cars operation was deliberately reduced to about 750,000 cars per annum which was not much more than half of the notional 1.2 million capacity of BL cars in 1977 (Edwardes, 1983, p. 65). By the time Sir Michael Edwardes left the company in 1982, the peripheral plants of Rover and Triumph at Speke, Canley and Solihull had been closed and production concentrated in the two central Austin Morris plants at Longbridge and Cowley. The Austin Morris assembly plant at Seneffe in Belgium was also closed. Edwardes himself described the recovery plan of 1977–80 as a plan for 'shrinking the business to a level beyond which we believed it was not safe to go' (Edwardes, 1983, p. 95). Essentially, the strategy was to turn the company into a relatively small-scale producer of volume cars for the mass market; the Austin Rover cars division which was created by the rationalisation programme of these years had a capacity which was not much more than half that of European majors (such as Fiat, Renault and VW) which could all produce at least 1.5 million cars a year.

The closures represented the more negative aspects. The strategy also had a positive side because the new managerial team aimed to establish the preconditions for a 'leaner and fitter' cars division which would be moderately profitable and highly productive. Ryder had planned a 'massive programme to modernise plant and equipment' at BL whereby £2,000 million was to be invested in cars and trucks over eight years with the government supplying all the funding in the early years. This emphasis on state-funded investment was carried over into the new strategy which reasserted the priority of major projects like the small car (Metro) which would be built on an automated body line at Longbridge. Inevitably, the total amount invested and the sources of funding were juggled around under the various recovery plans; the BL company finally obtained £2,100 million of public dividend capital and drew £1,500 million in private loans which were guaranteed by the state. In many ways, the main difference was that, after Michael Edwardes took over, the rationale for massive investment in new product and process technology inside the cars division was elaborated and made more explicit. The company finally decided to develop a compact model range centred on three new models (the Metro, Maestro, and Montego) which would be built to a high standard in new automated facilities. When the company had introduced a competitive model in each of the three main market classes (small, light and medium) then 'product-led recovery' should follow. On this scenario, the company's home market share would then rise above 20 per cent, export sales would increase and the new factories at Longbridge and Cowley would be loaded with throughput. By the time Sir Michael Edwardes left the company in 1982, the programme of new model launches was half completed. The small Metro, launched in October 1980, was followed into the marketplace by the light Maestro in April 1983 and the medium Montego in April 1984. As a stopgap expedient while the new light and medium cars were being developed, the company decided to assemble the Honda Ballade which was badged as the Triumph Acclaim when it was launched in October 1981. The company subsequently cooperated with Honda on the development of a large car which was launched as the Rover 800 in summer 1986.

If new product was essential for increased market share, the company assumed that this product could only be produced efficiently and profitably if the company invested in new process technology. Thus the two central manufacturing plants at Longbridge and Cowley were extensively and expensively retooled. Re-equipment was undertaken at a time when new automated techniques of car body building were becoming available to car producers and the company invested heavily in this new technology. The showpieces of the new strategy were two automated body lines at Longbridge and Cowley which cost the company nearly £300 million; the three new volume models (Metro, Maestro and Montego) were built on these new lines. It was always recognised that investment in new technology was futile if the company did not at the same time reform work practices. The Ryder team had taken a softly-softly approach to labour problems inside the firm; a complicated structure of committees promoted a process of worker participation and consultation which would co-opt the work-force and, if that failed, tranches of investment would be witheld to punish the work-force. The approach after 1977 was entirely different. The new strategy was to negotiate directly on work-practice reform and, when that failed, to wrest concessions from the work-force through conflict and confrontation. As Michael Edwardes saw it, the new management team faced the problem of 'tussling . . . with the militant shop stewards who controlled many of our factories' (Edwardes, 1983, p. 49). Though many criticised the management's tactics, there can be no doubt that they were successful in that management obtained a comprehensive reform of work practices; the struggle with the work-force culminated in management's successful unilateral imposition of new work practices in April 1980.

The post-1977 strategy therefore centred on three objectives — new product, new process technology and reform of work practices. As we have seen, the company achieved all three of these immediate objectives. The new models were launched (more or less on time); new technology was introduced and the work-force was effectively confronted. The question now must be whether this saved the company in the sense that it transformed market penetration, productive efficiency and financial results. It is important to remember that this kind of 'success' is defined largely in terms of enterprise goals: to enable BL to become an enterprise which could survive, with a reduced output and without the need for government subvention. Amongst the means adopted were mass redundancies and major abridgements of the effective rights of trade unions in the enterprise. It might well be argued that a 'success' with such costs hardly merits the name. Such a view raises vital issues of public policy. However, in this book we shall take the narrow criteria of 'success' as given. Our analysis is thus concerned with how far the recovery strategy did achieve the goals specified by the BL management: a significant improvement in market share, productive efficiency and financial results. From this perspective, the most generally accepted conclusion by the mid-1980s was that the strategy had been a qualified success.

Naturally enough, the principal author of the strategy more than endorsed this view. In his autobiography *Back from the Brink*, Sir Michael Edwardes claimed that the strategy had been a success. Investment in new technology and reform of work practices had produced major increases in efficiency; for example, after the production of the Metro began in the summer of 1980, 'the Longbridge factory began the climb in productivity which has taken it to the top of the European league' (Edwardes, 1983, p. 182). He recognised that the results in terms of output and sales were still disappointing. But in his autobiography, which was completed in 1983, this was attributed to the problem of 'product gap'. The company could not develop three new models at the same time and the launch of the light Maestro was delayed till 1983, with the medium Montego following in 1984; as he wrote, 'the 1980–1982 gap in the mid-car sector was the stuff from which nightmares are made' (Edwardes, 1983, p. 287). Sir Michael was then confident that when all the new models had been launched, market share would improve and 'in the mid-1980s the car operation should be profitable and secure' (Edwardes, 1983, p. 287). Thus, the initiator of the new strategy had few misgivings when he resigned as chairman in 1982: 'And so I leave a very hot seat with more to be done, but with a feeling that the foundations are now well and truly laid; and that the continuing patience and persistence of the Board and top management, together with the products that are in the pipeline, will complete the job' (Edwardes, 1983, p. 294).

In a qualified way, the optimism of Sir Michael Edwardes was independently confirmed by some of the academics who write about the car industry and its problems. The recent work of Daniel Jones (1985a; 1985b) conveys the impression that, in the Edwardes era, the company tackled major problems in a purposeful manner; that, as a result, performance had improved in productivity and in the market-place; and that success was clearly in sight. Writing in 1984, Jones projected that, with the benefit of new models, Austin Rover would sell 575,000 cars in 1986; if that sales volume were achieved, it would represent a 62 per cent volume increase on 1982 production levels (Bessant *et al.*, 1984, p. 23). For a more sustained treatment of the company's problems, we can turn to Willman and Winch's (1985) monograph on the reform of labour relations at BL in the late 1970s and early 1980s. In this scholarly work, Willman and Winch recognise that the company has had problems with the market for cars, but they suppose that the post-1977 strategy successfully transformed the company's position and prospects. By the late 1970s, BL was 'in a serious spiral of decline' and now (1984) 'one could argue that the spiral of decline has been reversed' (Willman and Winch, 1985, p. 41). They claim that one of their chapters 'illustrates the emergence of a successful strategic approach to the company's problems in the Edwardes era' (Willman and Winch, 1985, p. 42). A similar academic verdict was contained in another work written from the different perspective of political science. 'By 1 October 1982 when Edwardes stepped down as executive Chairman, BL prospects looked hopeful and, with the highly successful launch of the Maestro in March 1983, the company seemed a better bet than at any time since 1975' (Wilks, 1984, p. 205).

In the spring of 1986, the question of Austin Rover's success became a lively political issue when it was disclosed that the government was talking with Ford and attempting to privatise the division by selling it to another car company. Austin Rover defended itself by publishing a series of advertisements, one of which was headed 'Austin Rover. The truth.' (*Observer*, 16 February 1986). The advert emphasised the role of the cars division in the UK economy: 'We employ 38,000 people in the United Kingdom'; 'overseas sales earned Britain £300 million' in 1985; and Austin Rover 'had a larger share of the European car market than either Mercedes or BMW'. But the advert also emphasised the achievements of the company in terms of output and efficiency. In 1985 'total output of cars grew by 22%' and 'We had 14% increase in export sales'. The company claimed to be amongst the world leaders in application of new technology and asserted that 'our technology and our productivity are now amongst the best in the world'; further, an 'independent survey shows that we have the most efficient production-line in Europe at our Longbridge factory'. Critical readers will notice some curious omissions. The advert made no mention of the company's financial record in terms of profit and loss. The claims about output and exports are also difficult to interpret when the company did not give a run of figures for five or ten years. Moreover, the point of comparison in the advert is 1984 when the company's performance was particularly poor. But the interesting point is that the company's claims were widely accepted. Most politicians in the mid-1980s endorsed what they regarded as a substantial achievement. Edward Heath could, on this topic, be taken as expressing a considered and informed view when he pronounced that 'we should . . . take pride in what has been done to help BL bring about a remarkable turn-round in its fortunes at a time of world depression' (*Observer*, 6 April 1986).

The claims made by Austin Rover Group (ARG) and BL management have thus been widely accepted. This acceptance was understandable in 1983 or 1984 before the new model range was complete; it was then plausible to argue, as Sir Michael Edwardes did, that the best was yet to come and the first signs were promising. When we now have the results for the period up to and including 1985, it is clear that Michael Edwardes was indulging in wishful thinking and that the later claims by Austin Rover management were frankly disingenuous. Any systematic review of the division's market, productive and financial performance suggests that the claims of progress cannot now be justified. Most of the issues will be discussed in greater detail in later chapters, so we will here concentrate on the basics, beginning with a consideration of the claims about output and sales.

The fundamental point about output and sales is that 'product-led recovery' never happened. Table 1.1 summarises the relevant statistics. Austin Rover's output was never increased much above the low level

Table 1.1. Austin Rover production, home sales and exports 1978–85

Year	Production[1] (000s)	Export allocation (000s)	Percentage of output exported	UK sales (000s)	Total UK market (000s)	ARG market share[2] (%)
1978	611.6	247.9	40.5	373.8	1591.9	23.5
1979	503.8	200.2	39.7	337.0	1716.3	19.6
1980	395.8	157.8	39.9	275.8	1513.8	18.2
1981	413.4	126.2	30.5	285.1	1484.7	19.2
1982	383.1	133.9	35.0	277.3	1555.0	17.8
1983	445.4	118.3	26.6	332.7	1791.7	18.6
1984	383.3	78.6	20.5	312.1	1749.7	17.8
1985	465.1	—	—	328.0	1832.4	17.9

Source: SMMT, *Annual Statistics*

1. Includes Jaguar for all years except 1984 and 1985 (Jaguar production in 1980 was 15,469, rising to 25,467 in 1983) because comparable figures to subtract from exports are not available.
2. Includes Austin Morris, Rover and Triumph, but from 1980 excludes Jaguar (1978–9 figures include some 5,000 or 6,000 Jaguar saloons).

of around 450,000 cars which was the norm for volume cars in the late 1970s. Clearly part of the problem was caused by the collapse in export volumes in the late 1970s; after 1981 exports fluctuated at or below 100,000 cars and showed no steady upward trend despite the introduction of new models. As a proportion of output, exports slumped from the near 40 per cent level which was steadily maintained in the 1970s to around 20 per cent in the mid-1980s. There was a modest recovery in output levels after 1980 when the company only made just over 300,000 cars. This limited recovery in output arose entirely from an expansion of domestic sales on a British car market which was recovering quite strongly from a cyclical slump in demand for cars. More significant and less encouraging is the fact that the company's *share* of the domestic market was not increased dramatically and remained well short of 20 per cent. The Metro was launched in October 1980 and so for most of that year Austin Rover was selling a range of old models, which claimed 18 per cent of the market. By 1985, the division had three new models (Metro, Maestro and Montego) on sale for the full year and yet the company could still only win 18 per cent of the market. For a long period the company had ambitious plans to increase output and production was scheduled to increase to 535,000 in 1985 and 575,000 in 1986 (*The Engineer*, 19 April 1984). From our analysis it will be seen that these plans were unrealistic and an increase of production by 60,000 cars in the first half of 1985 simply left the company with large stocks of unsold motor cars (*Financial Times*, 23 August 1985).

The company's claim about increases in labour productivity raises complicated issues of concepts and definition which will be addressed in Chapter 2. We argue that the most relevant measure of overall efficiency is that which relates total car output to the total work-force employed in all the Austin Rover factories. The large-scale redundancies of the early 1980s might have been expected to increase this overall labour productivity substantially. But the 11.6 cars per man year of 1985, whilst it represented an improvement on the low levels of the late 1970s, did not raise labour productivity hugely above the levels which had been achieved in the early 1970s. In 1972 Austin Morris made 698,000 cars with 80,000 workers and, without the benefit of robots, showed a labour productivity of 8.7 cars per man (Williams *et al.*, 1983, p. 255). Moreover, the 11.6 cars per man of 1985 remains unexceptional by European standards. The fundamental point is that work-practice reform and automation have not paid off in terms of a huge increase in divisional labour productivity. It should also be noted that, when new technology is introduced, capital productivity is an important measure of overall efficiency and it is misleading to concentrate exclusively on labour productivity. As we argue in Chapter 3, the divisional record on capital productivity is much worse than the record on labour productivity; at every level and by any measure, capital productivity deteriorated substantially as new technology was introduced.

The one area where the company made apparent progress was in the control of operating losses. BL Cars (which included Austin Rover) made huge losses in the early 1980s; in the worst year, 1980, the company made a trading loss of £271 million. But within three years, the trading loss had been converted into a small profit of £2.7 million and, although the results in later years have again worsened, they have not worsened very much. This performance was creditable when most European volume car manufacturers were losing money and some were losing very large sums of money; Renault lost £1,000 million in 1984 and again in 1985. None the less, it is perhaps not surprising that Austin Rover's adverts were silent about the division's financial performance because the improvement here was more apparent than real. The issues here are technical and they are discussed in an appendix at the end of this book. This appendix concludes that Austin Rover's profitability was improved by the way in which the division took low depreciation allowances and operated within a funding framework which minimised the burden of interest charges on the division. If the division had made realistic depreciation provision and paid interest on the funds which it had borrowed from its parent, then the company would at a conservative estimate still have been running up annual losses well in excess of £100 million.

By the measures of financial, productive and market achievement, the recovery programme has not been successful. The rest of our book examines the aims, achievement and performance of the enterprise in all three areas; the more the evidence is examined, the more we are forced to conclude that the division (or its equivalent in the 1986 reorganisation of the enterprise) is unlikely to be able to continue in its present form as a manufacturer of volume cars. However, our main interest is not so much in the fact of failure as in its causes, which we attribute to managerial miscalculation. Our thesis is that Austin Rover and BL management inadequately appreciated the constraints imposed upon them by the economics of car manufacture and by the limits laid down by the circumstances in which the business operated. Through an analysis of the managerial miscalculation, we aim to produce a case study in the failure of business strategy.

Given this broad objective, the organisation of the book is mostly obvious and straightforward. The post-1977 strategy had three major objectives: reform of work practices; introduction of new technology; and development of new models to win increased market share. Each major objective is dealt with in a separate chapter: Chapter 2 deals with the labour problem and reform of work practices; Chapter 3 examines investment strategy and the introduction of new technology; and Chapter 4 analyses the market for cars. In all three areas, we argue that management made crucial miscalculations. The labour problem was unreasonably privileged and a disproportionate effort went into the reform of work practices which was a necessary but not a sufficient condition for creating a more productive and profitable enterprise. On investment, the physical and financial return on investment in new technology was disappointing partly because the company made inappropriate decisions about the choice of new technology and invested in inflexibility. The strategy of creating a much smaller volume car company was always an inherently risky one because, as we argue, the economies of scale still operate powerfully in the cars division. In any case, as our chapter on markets shows, the output of the smaller company could not be sold and this created major problems in a high fixed-cost business. The division overestimated the number of cars it could sell because it did not sufficiently recognise the powerful market limitations which operated against the company in its efforts to sell cars at home and abroad.

In an earlier essay on the problems of BMC and BLMC (Williams *et al.*, 1983) it was argued that the failure of these companies was caused by problems with the market for cars. It is now argued that Austin Rover's problems on the home market became more acute with a change in the form of competition in the early and mid-1980s. There was the renaissance of Vauxhall, which matched Ford and Austin Rover by introducing a full range of competitive models. The effect was to make sales in each market class more fragmented so that the volume which could be obtained at home with a compact model range was necessarily limited. Export sales were the only way out for Austin Rover but, as we will show, the company failed to develop export markets. At the same time our argument about market-led failure is set in the context of a broader discussion about the gains from reform of work practices and from the introduction of new technology. Even if the company had consistently made sound decisions on these issues, the return on effort would have been relatively small as long as market limitations continued to operate. The fundamental strategic miscalculation of the Edwardes team was to suppose that the key problems were inside the company and, therefore, Austin Rover's future depended on what it did itself by way of tackling the internal problems of product, process technology and labour productivity. Against this, we would argue that the basic problem was outside the division in the market-place, where Austin Rover was beset by market limitations which could only have been sufficiently modified by political action.

Our aim has been to produce a case study of the failure of business strategy and industrial policy. The larger issues about the role of government policy are taken up in our fifth and concluding chapter. This chapter begins by establishing some broader connections; it argues that the miscalculations of the Austin Rover management and the market predicament of the firm are typical of many others in British manufacturing. Our case study can therefore focus public concern about issues which are of general importance for the future of British manufacturing. The broader theme is more fully discussed elsewhere (Cutler *et al.*, 1986) but on the specific issue of Austin Rover and motor cars, we do not consider that we are unnecessarily provoking our readers by choosing the title 'breakdown of Austin Rover'. Indeed, in an important sense, the title has become a more or less literal description. When the government installed a new management team at BL in May 1986, one of its early actions was to change the name of the company. The company as a whole became the Rover Group and its cars division ceased therefore to be known as Austin Rover. But beyond this our title is justified by the conviction (which the book aims to substantiate) that we have reached a crisis point where the survival of Austin Rover as a volume car manufacturer, (or indeed the survival of a substantial car manufacturing sector in Britain) is unlikely as long as present (1986) government policies continue. On present trends, the assembly of imported kits must replace the manufacture of British cars. Our final chapter shows that this outcome would be disastrous; Britain needs the employment, value added and export sales which Austin Rover, and the other enterprises in cars and car components, can only generate through manufacture. At the same time, we believe that neither the particular enterprise nor the cars industry as a whole need be scrapped; the enterprise and the industry can start and run again as an engine of prosperity if government policies are changed. Our final chapter concludes with a proposal for new kinds of government intervention, which would safeguard the domestic market by giving some preference to those enterprises which manufacture British cars rather than assemble foreign kits.

2 / The Labour Problem?

In the mid-1970s there were several major official inquiries into the decline of the British car industry. The House of Commons Expenditure Committee (1975) and the Central Policy Review Staff (1975) both in rather different ways blamed the problems of the industry on underinvestment and bad work practices. The Ryder Report (1975) into the collapse of BLMC concurred. Michael Edwardes was brought in as chairman when Ryder's expansionist solution of massive public investment in a nationalised car company which would make a million cars a year had failed. But the Edwardes team accepted the conventional secondary understanding of the problems of the company and the industry. Although they introduced a rationalisation programme of closures and sackings, many of the strategic projects and priorities of the previous top management were endorsed. In particular, the new team took over the plans for massive investment in new automated production facilities which would build new models like the Metro. From this point of view, labour appeared to be a crucial problem, even *the* crucial problem, for BL management in the late 1970s. The Central Policy Review Staff (CRPS) had shown that labour productivity in the UK car industry was around 30 per cent lower than in France, Italy and West Germany and that, within the British industry, BLMC's performance was significantly worse than that of Ford (Willman and Winch, 1985, p. 28). More to the point, the CPRS had shown that bad work practices obstructed efficient capital utilisation in British car factories. Process comparisons showed that British car firms needed more labour than their European counterparts to make the same product using similar or identical capital equipment to that in European factories. Reform of work practices could thus be plausibly represented as a prerequisite for the efficient use of the sophisticated new capital equipment which the company was buying in with the aid of government funding.

This was certainly the view taken by senior BL management in the Edwardes era. They believed that there was a series of interrelated 'labour problems' inside the company about work practices and manning levels which cost the company a lot of money. In management's view these problems had their origins in the nature and scope of the collective bargaining arrangements inside the company. The company had a two-tier bargaining system for negotiating pay and conditions. Basic pay was determined in annual negotiations between the company and a committee which brought together the eleven unions representing the company's hourly-paid workers. More specific terms and conditions were then negotiated on a lower tier at plant and workshop level. Changes in work practice and the introduction of new technology had to be negotiated on a shop-by-shop basis with the plant stewards who were the unofficial elected representatives of the work-force. At this lowest level, the workers had established wide prerogatives. For example, the transfer of workers inside the plant generally required prior discussion between management, supervisors and shop stewards. More significantly, the so-called principle of 'mutuality' required that any change in work practices (work methods, manning levels or time allowances) could not be introduced by management before it had obtained the consent of the stewards (Willman and Winch, 1985, pp. 67, 113, 126). Under the principle of mutuality, new technology would thus have to stand idle until the stewards had accepted management's proposals for manning levels and work-pace.

The problems had long been perceived. Previous managements had put considerable effort into the reform of collective bargaining; in the early 1970s, measured day work was introduced as a substitute for piece work and the Ryder report formalised the objective of reducing the number of bargaining units. Although these changes might have reduced the likelihood of strikes over wage rates and wage differentials, the company was still, when Michael Edwardes took over, in a position where changes in work practice (with or without new technology) had to be locally negotiated within a framework where the status quo was always maintained until change was acceptable to the stewards. Furthermore, the management felt that the strike weapon allowed the work-force to 'blackmail' them whenever the process of negotiation was not producing acceptable results. In management's view, the work-force walked off the job unreasonably often. Michael Edwardes recalls that in 1977 the daily 'dispute list' provided for senior management often ran to five sheets (Edwardes, 1983, p. 14). The situation was not much better in the following year 1978: 'Although disputes were well down on 1977, there were nevertheless 346 disputes which had disrupted the flow of production. The overwhelming majority were wildcat strikes — unofficial strikes which embarrassed the more responsible union officials who knew their own authority, as well as management's was being challenged' (Edwardes, 1983, p. 78). In the management view, local (unofficial) bargaining had assumed an excessive role and the corporate system of industrial relations ceded too much power to unofficial union representatives at workshop level. It was in this context that management formulated its industrial relations strategy for the cars division.

It was accepted that the unions, especially the bureaucracy of national and local officials, had a valuable role to play in negotiating annual pay settlements. The company quickly decided that the unions would have to accept low pay rises; single figure pay rises below the rate of inflation meant that the work-force was being asked to accept real wage cuts. But that was a tough negotiating position which did not diminish the company's commitment to institutionalised collective bargaining at the national level with officials who were seen as the legitimate representatives of all the company's workers. What management wanted to do was to abolish unofficial local union and shop steward control over work practices; manning levels, work-pace and the organisation of work would be re-established as the sole prerogative of management and the scope of collective bargaining would be narrowed because these matters would cease to be negotiable. Stewards would find their proper role in the administration of the company procedures which would, in the new order, deal with worker grading and job grievances. In neo-Marxist terminology, management aimed to reassert its control over the labour process; or, in the jargon of industrial relations, management strategy was about changing the terms of the effort bargain. BL management saw the issue in quasi-Thatcherite terms as a matter of asserting 'management's right to manage'. The imperative need to introduce new technology on management's terms was wrapped up in a broader managerial philosophy. As a key company document on work practices claimed, 'It is managers who have the responsibility for managing, leading and motivating employees and for communicating on company welfare' (1980 *Blue Newspaper*, quoted in Willman and Winch, 1985, p. 130). The message for the work-force was that henceforth they would be led by managers rather than stewards.

On the industrial relations front, management pursued its strategic objective in a style which some praised as robust and daring and others damned as macho and provocative. For management the labour problem was so important that it was worth taking the company to the brink, or over the brink if the work-force would not accept what management said was necessary. The weakness of the company then became a major strength for management. In negotiations on a variety of issues, management insisted that, if its terms were not accepted, the company might fold altogether or government would withdraw financial support or management would not feel justified in asking for additional government assistance. For example, in 1980 and 1981 when the cars work-force threatened to strike over low pay offers, management responded with the promise that the factories would then close permanently. The pressure on union negotiators at every level was increased by management's repeated use of the device of direct ballots of the work-force. For example, in September–October 1979, 80 per cent of the work-force voted in favour of the Edwardes 'recovery plan' which provided a charter for subsequent closures and sackings. This undermined the position of Derek Robinson, the chief steward at Longbridge, who was sacked in a highly symbolic way in November 1979 for refusing to recant his public opposition to the recovery plan. From management's point of view, the issue of reformed work practices was the most delicate and important labour relations issue. On this management finally decided to impose new work practices unilaterally; any employee reporting for work on 8 or 9 April 1980 was deemed to have accepted the company's new conditions of work.

In his autobiography, Michael Edwardes claimed that 'from the start, everything we did in employee relations was tested against the broad strategy of regaining management control' (Edwardes, 1983, p. 181). By this narrow standard the reform of industrial relations was a considerable success. From April 1980 onwards, management had virtually complete control over work practices; Willman and Winch noted that on the new Metro facility, 'trade union control of manning levels and of workspeeds had disappeared almost completely' (Willman and Winch, 1985, p. 170). Longbridge management was even able to select workers with suitable attitudes for jobs on the new Metro line. In recent years effort levels at Austin Rover have been determined by management's own industrial engineers and the plant-level productivity bonuses which the company pays are non-negotiable. It is a substantial achievement that such major changes were obtained without provoking the response of a major strike at Longbridge and Cowley. Indeed, under the new regime of industrial relations, Austin Rover was significantly more strike-free than it had been before. As Table 2.1 shows, the BL company, as a

Table 2.1. Man hours lost through strikes[1] at BL as a percentage of total available man hours

1977	5.9
1978	3.5
1979	5.1
1980	1.5
1981	1.6
1982	1.6
1983	1.0
1984	4.0
1985	0.05.

Source: BL Annual Report and Accounts and BL Corporate Plan, various years (1984 and 1985 figures supplied by BL).

1. A strike is an internal stoppage of one hour or more.

whole, typically lost just 1.5 per cent of available man hours through strikes in the 1980s compared with an average of around 5 per cent in the late 1970s. Management probably exaggerated the extent to which the company had suffered from strikes in the late 1970s; by the company's own measure it was 95 per cent strike-free in the worst years of the late 1970s and the strikes which did occur often lost output which was not readily saleable. But management's rhetorical exaggeration of its own achievement does not detract from its reality. The record on strikes in the 1980s is all the more impressive because management insisted on low pay settlements which averaged around 5.5 per cent in each year from 1978 to 1983. This policy was in practice softened when management paid significant plant-level productivity bonuses. From 1978 to 1982 basic pay increased by 22 per cent while, over a slightly different period, from 1977 to 1982 hourly employees' gross pay increased by 77 per cent (Centre for Policy Studies, 1983, p. 32). Generous bonuses could, of course, be justified on the grounds that they represented the pay-back on a real improvement in efficiency which workers had earned through accepting reformed work practices.

The company has made large claims about improvements in efficiency and consistently implied that these improvements were caused by a reform of work practices which reinforced the effects of investment in new technology. In his published account, Sir Michael Edwardes summarised the position after the April 1980 imposition of new work practices.

> Thirty years of management concessions which made it impossible to manufacture cars competitively were thrown out of the window and our

> car factories found themselves with a fighting chance of becoming more competitive. The results were not long in coming through, productivity which had declined steadily over the years leapt up. In 1980 Longbridge produced 7 cars a man. With the new working practices progressively introduced alongside the new Metro facility, productivity in 1981 rose to nearly 17 cars a man and continued through to 1982 when it exceeded 25 cars a man (Edwardes, 1983, p. 128).

He then claimed that these improvements had taken Longbridge 'to the top of the European league' in terms of productivity and this showed. 'what a public sector workforce can do when led by a properly motivated and confident management' (Edwardes, 1983, pp. 182, 252). The company's productivity showpiece was the new automated Metro line in the Longbridge plant. In 1981, Michael Edwardes told the Commons Trade and Industry Committee that when the Metro line was commissioned in 1980 productivity was 14.8 cars per man year and by January 1981 this had increased to 29.5 cars per man year, which was 'comparable with the best European practice' (House of Commons Select Committee on Trade and Industry Committee, 1981, Q. 221). By 1985, Harold Musgrove, then chairman of Austin Rover, tightened up the claims another notch or two by asserting that only thirty-three labour hours went into making a Metro which 'is a performance I would challenge anyone, anywhere in the world to beat' (*Financial Times*, 12 January 1985).

Predictably, the media hailed all this as a 'productivity miracle' (see, for example, *Sunday Times*, 21 March 1982). More significantly, management's claims were corroborated in studies carried out by independent researchers. Austin Rover proudly advertised that 'a recent independent survey shows we have the most efficient production-line in Europe at our Longbridge plant' (*Observer*, 16 February 1986). The company was referring to the results of a survey by *The Engineer* (9 February 1984) which compared productivity in three processes (body in white, paint and final assembly) on the Metro line at Longbridge with productivity in similar processes at various European plants (see Table 2.2). In process productivity terms, Austin Rover's performance was the best in Europe. Furthermore, in a recent monograph on the reform of industrial relations at Austin Rover in the early 1980s, Willman and Winch (1985) do not doubt the company's claims. It is sometimes difficult to follow their argument about productivity, but it is clear that they accept there was a substantial improvement in

Table 2.2. Comparison of European productivity in three processes[1]

Manufacturer	Works	Model	Cars per man year
Austin Rover	Longbridge	Metro	55.5
Peugeot	Mulhouse	205	54.7
Fiat	Rivalta	Uno/Strada	50.5
Ford	Saarlouis	Escort/Orion	49.9
VW	Wolfsburg	Polo/Golf	45.9
Renault	Flins	R9/11	38.0
Talbot	Ryton	Horizon/Alpine Solara	37.6
Ford	Halewood	Escort/Orion	26.2

Source: *The Engineer*, 9 February 1984.

1. Body in white, paint and final assembly.

productivity and show that this was not an automatic consequence of the introduction of new technology on the Metro lines. Willman and Winch demonstrate that significant productivity improvements preceded the introduction of new technology and such improvements were obtained on lines where new technology was not used (Willman and Winch, 1985, pp. 151–5).

These management claims and research results appear to provide a triumphant vindication of the company's industrial relations strategy. But anyone who is interested in exact measurement and precise attribution will find much that is unsatisfactory and blurred in these claims about productivity improvement. For example, only *The Engineer* survey explicitly includes all direct and indirect hourly-paid workers. Some of the other claims must refer only to direct labour in some processes. The Musgrove claim that it took only 33 man hours to make a Metro cannot be accepted at face value since it was made at a time when it took the clever Japanese all of 140 man hours to produce a motor car (Altshuler, 1984, p. 160). Amidst all this confusion, one point is very clear, the company chooses to emphasise only labour productivity (cars per man year) and prefers to measure that at the lower operating levels (process, line or plant). In their nature, all these measures are problematic indicators of efficiency.

Process productivity is a particularly dubious guide because high labour productivity in one or two processes can always be bought by selective investment in those processes. In this context, it is significant that the body welding, body in white and paint processes which featured in the new Metro claims are the three processes where virtually all of Austin Rover's investment was concentrated. Measures relating to a particular model line are more significant, but only if the length of the line and the span of processes included in the measure are carefully defined. This was never done by company spokesmen. For example, it is not clear whether the Metro line claims include the process of power train production. This is relevant because the scope for reducing labour input in power train production must have been limited when the A series engines for the Metro were being made on transfer lines which are thirty years old. Plant-level productivity, which is emphasised by Edwardes, is again a dubious measure. Assembly-plant productivity is a function of the model mix produced at the plant; the introduction of new higher-volume models and/or the transfer of lower-volume models to a particular assembly plant will automatically improve productivity at one plant. In the early 1980s, Longbridge benefited from both effects; the Mini was retained in production at Longbridge where the Metro, a new high-volume small car, was introduced and, in due course, the low volume Acclaim was also transferred from Longbridge to Cowley.

If there are problems with measuring labour productivity at process, line or plant level, our major point is the rather different one that these measures of performance at the lower operating levels are, in the nature of things, inappropriate measures of company performance. Austin Rover cannot survive by selling bodies in white, or by manufacturing the one Metro model or by operating the one assembly plant at Longbridge. The measure of company performance which really matters is the higher-level company one which relates total Austin Rover car production to the total work-force in all the car division factories, which include not only the two major assembly plants at Longbridge and Cowley but also a pressings plant at Swindon and components plants, like the one at Llanelli, which feeds both assembly plants.

When labour productivity is measured at the company level, Austin Rover's performance can be related to the achievement of other European car companies and also to the achievement of the Austin Morris volume car business in the 1970s. The results of this comparison are pretty dispiriting, which is no doubt why they were seldom mentioned by company spokesmen. After the miracle, in 1983 Austin Rover employed 41,000 workers and manufactured around 433,000 cars per annum; the division in 1983 thus achieved a performance of 10.6 cars per man year and the company has not managed any significant improvement since then. In relative European terms this is mediocre; all the major European manufacturers were making 11–15 cars per man year in the later 1970s before the present round of investment in automation got under way (Hartley, 1981, p. 137). It is sometimes argued that such intra-company comparisons are invalid because different manufacturers buy in more or less of their cars in component form. To guard against distortion, it would be reasonable to make the comparison with the company's own performance in earlier periods. At Austin Rover, the proportion of bought-in components has increased with the introduction of the Triumph Acclaim, which is built from kits of Honda parts, and the incorporation of bought-in major mechanicals like VW and Honda gearboxes into the Maestro and Montego. When the company is making less of the car in-house, this should flatter Austin Rover's performance. But even with this assistance the company's mid-1980s performance did not compare particularly favourably with past achievements. As Table 2.3 shows, in the bad old days of underinvestment and unreformed work practices, the Austin Morris volume cars division of BLMC achieved a best performance of 8.7 cars per man year in 1972 from the same factories as Austin Rover occupied in the 1980s.

When the comparison is extended further back, the conclusions about long-run trends are even more striking. The old BMC company, whose output mix included trucks and tractors as well as cars, managed a best-ever productivity performance of 9.2 vehicles per man year in 1963–4; the implication is that productivity in the Austin and Morris car factories was, twenty years earlier, possibly higher than it was in 1983 (Williams *et al.*, 1983, p. 222). A figure of 10.6 cars per man year does not represent a significant long-run improvement on the achieved performance of the early 1960s. Of course, modern cars are increasingly complex and loaded with 'extras' like electric windows and central locking which all have to be fitted on the assembly line. But that consideration hardly excuses Austin Rover's performance because most of the company's output consists of cheap cars with fairly basic specifications. Leaving the interpretative niceties aside, the basic fact is that the secular long-run trend of labour productivity inside the company was flat for more than twenty years. And this conclusion contradicts the impression created by the company's claims which imply substantial progress on the labour productivity front.

If we wish to take the argument further, it is necessary to distinguish between long- and short-run labour productivity trends. As we have just argued, the Edwardes miracle did no more than return

Table 2.3. Volume car labour productivity at Austin Morris and Austin Rover, 1969–85[1]

(a) Austin Morris volume cars

	Production (000s)	Employees (000s)	Cars per man year
1969	634	81	7.8
1970	588	88	6.7
1971	666	81	8.2
1972	698	80	8.7
1973	673	85	7.9
1974	561	81	6.9
1975	450	81	5.6

(b) Austin Morris and BL Components[2]

	Production	Employees	Cars per man year
1978	466	86	5.4
1979	348	81	4.3

(c) Austin Rover

	Production	Employees[3]	Cars per man year
1980	315		
1981	348	77	4.5
1982	370	48	7.7
1983	433	41	10.6
1984	390	42	9.3

Sources: (a) BLMC Annual Reports, 1969–75
(b) BL Annual Report, 1970–80
(c) ARG Annual Reports, 1980–4

1. Because of corporate reorganization it is impossible to present one continuous series. The different series are reasonably comparable because Austin Morris and Austin Rover both produced cars from two central assembly plants (Longbridge and Cowley) and associated satellite factories which supply components.
2. 'BL Components' includes the Unipart spare parts merchandising operation and SU Butec, which manufactured carburettors and fuel pumps. According to the 1980 BL Report, BL Components then employed 7,000 workers. This information, and the similarity in employment totals in (a) and (b), suggests that productivity figures for 1978 and 1979 are reasonably comparable with those for earlier years.
3. This is a total of the average number of employees through the year taken from the ARG accounts lodged in Companies House. When the company was shedding workers in the early 1980s the basis of measurement was of some importance. Lower end-of-year employee counts would improve the cars per man year result. The 1981 employee total in the ARG accounts seems suspiciously high. According to the BL Report, 'car operations' (including Jaguar, Rover and Triumph) shed 24,200 men in 1980 and Austin Rover 12,000 in 1981. The BL Reports suggest that the shedding of manpower began a year or so before 1981. This uncertainty about chronology does not affect our general argument.

the company to the labour productivity standards which had long been average for the industry and which the company had itself achieved twenty years previously. Nevertheless, as Table 2.3 shows, the miracle did represent a significant short-run recovery in productivity standards; from a nadir of around 4.0 cars per man year in 1978–9 labour productivity increased to 10.6 cars per man year in 1983. This short-run recovery is dramatic enough and can be applauded. But the question we must now ask is: what role did the Edwardes strategy play in generating the short-run revival of the early 1980s? Cyclical short-run variations in labour productivity, albeit of a less pronounced sort, had long been a feature of the volume cars business. In the 1950s and 1960s, BMC productivity varied between 5.9 and 9.2 vehicles per man year. And, in the first half of the 1970s, Austin Morris productivity varied between 5.5 and 8.7 cars per man year. When the miracle is set in this context, as one more short-run fluctuation, another important point emerges. The company has implied, and public discussion has accepted, that reformed work practices and new technology were the dominant causes of the productivity improvement in the early 1980s. But, from Table 2.3, it is quite clear that the relation between production volumes and the number of employees is the crucial determinant of short-run changes in productivity in the early 1980s as in previous periods. When the causes of the recent short-run recovery are analysed in these terms, the achievement of Austin Rover management becomes much less heroic than its presentation would suggest.

If there are two variables in the productivity equation (production volume and numbers employed), shifts in either variable have entirely predictable results. In the short (and long) run, as long as the work-force is constant, declines in production volume automatically depress productivity. This is as true from one year to another in Austin Rover in the 1980s as it was in Austin Morris in the 1970s. Thus, when production declined from 433,000 cars in 1983 to 390,000 cars in 1984, the number of cars per man year produced fell by 1.3; there were very similar year-on-year falls in productivity when sales fell, for example, from 1974 to 1975 or 1978 to 1979. The productivity problem which confronted the Edwardes team was created by a sustained fall of output to permanently lower levels after 1973; Austin Morris made nearly 700,000 volume cars a year in 1972 and 1973 but output declined to 450,000 cars in 1975 and thereafter remained at or below this level. With the work-force in volume cars roughly constant, this permanent loss of output inevitably compromised productivity; from a peak of 8.7 cars per man year when 80,000 workers made nearly 700,000 cars in 1972, productivity declined towards 4 cars per man year when a similar number of workers made 350,000 cars per year in 1979 and 1980. If the fall in volume car output created the productivity problem, management tackled it by adjusting the other variable in the equation and reducing the size of the work-force. As long as production is constant, any short-run reduction in the work-force automatically improves productivity. Closure of peripheral plants and slimming down of the central plants reduced the Austin Rover work-force from around 80,000 at the end of the 1970s to just 41,000 in 1983. The short-run improvement in productivity which occurred in these years was therefore substantially produced by a policy of wholesale sacking which brought the work-force into line with a much reduced output.

By the early 1980s, the company was making about half the number of cars it had made ten years previously; the company then shed half the work-force and the company ended up more or less where it was originally in terms of labour productivity. Neither new technology nor reform of work practices was a necessary precondition for this achievement. On the industrial relations front, the key precondition was established by the work-force ballot on the 'recovery plan' in autumn 1979; once the work-force had accepted the plan, the possibility of subsequent resistance to closure and sacking was undermined. The introduction of labour-displacing new technology in the central plants made it easier to remove some of the workers. But, as Willman and Winch show, there were substantial reductions in manning levels on the old traditional lines. Reformed work practices helped with this but were irrelevant to the closure of peripheral plants which was a major source of labour saving. In any case, the special factors of new technology and work-practice reform cannot have provided a unique dynamic because, by the measure of results, the achievement in adjusting the company's work-force to output levels was not unprecedented. Although half the work-force was removed, Michael Edwardes only reduced the work-force in line with the reduction in output; that is to say, he did no better — though in a reverse direction — than Len Lord and George Harriman of the old BMC, who in the 1950s and 1960s increased their work-force in line with the increase in output (Williams *et al.*, 1983, p. 222). The argument so far leads towards a revisionist conlusion. By the standard of achieved performance at company level, Austin Rover's labour productivity record does not show much sign of a substantial improvement which could be said to have reflected the successful introduction of new technology and work-practice reform.

At the same time it must be admitted that everything could still have come good if Austin Rover could have made and sold more motor cars. The company could therefore argue that the changes in work practice should be judged not by the standard of achieved company labour productivity performance, but by the standard of potential productivity performance. Earlier managements could and did use the excuse that they could have made more cars with the same number of workers in the right circumstances. In 1972, Austin Morris claimed that it lost 20 per cent of its output through strikes (House of Commons Expenditure Committee, 1975, p. 432); and, if that claim were accepted, it would imply a potential best performance of around 11 cars per man year in Austin Morris in the early 1970s. But, with the benefit of new technology and reformed work practices, Austin Rover in the mid-1980s had the potential to reach levels of productivity which Austin Morris could not. It is not clear just how many more cars Austin Rover could then have made without hiring more workers. Since a substantial proportion of the company's 750,000 capacity had not been used for some years, it must be doubtful whether Austin Rover had the balanced facilities to produce that number of cars. But the factories could certainly have produced 600,000 cars a year and that output would have given labour productivity of around 15 cars per man year. The problem is that, as Chapter 4 will argue, Austin Rover sales were powerfully constrained by market limitations and, if output could not be expanded for that reason, then the potential labour productivity improvement at the company level could not have been realised.

In this situation, in so far as new technology and reformed work practices do produce significant improvements in labour productivity at line or process level, the results simply embarrass the company. In 1981 there were lay-offs and extended holiday breaks on the Metro line which were then attributed to the fact that the Metro had not yet been launched into Europe. In 1985, the company increased production in the first six months of the year, accumulated unsaleable stocks of all three volume models and then announced there would be 200 redundancies on the Metro line plus a 10 per cent reduction in production schedules and an extra fortnight's shutdown on the Metro and Maestro–Montego lines (*Financial Times*, 20 August 1985). With company sales pressing against market limitations, the company's overall labour productivity performance is output-constrained and the workers on its most productive lines and processes are literally working themselves out of a job.

The discussion so far has concentrated on the issue of labour productivity, but if we are considering the consequences of reformed work practices, capital productivity is just as relevant as a measure of physical efficiency. Indeed, it is arguably more important because, as Willman and Winch argue, when the company sought changes in work practices before the Metro was introduced, 'the prime goal of the changes was . . . to ensure continuous production on the facility as a whole' (Willman and Winch, 1985, p. 183). Changes in work practice were only means to the end of the efficient use of capital equipment. Capital productivity is another issue about which management keeps quiet, and with very good reason. The company's record on capital utilisation at the line, plant and company level is not uneven or relatively mediocre; it is consistently appalling. We will reserve a technical discussion of capital productivity for the next chapter on Austin Rover's investment strategy. But we must observe now that the simple arithmetic of persistent overcapacity at company and line level in the 1980s ensures that 'continuous production on the facility as a whole' can never be achieved. As the next chapter demonstrates, during 1980–5 the company built an average of 423,000 cars a year in its two major plants (Longbridge and Cowley) which have a nominal two-shift capacity of 750,000 cars. Furthermore, at a line level, the company has never built more than 175,000 Metros a year on a facility which could turn out 400,000 cars a year. In this situation, the reform of work practices becomes, in overall productivity terms, a pointless exercise.

The conclusion must be that the company won its chosen battle about manning levels and work practices but lost the war which was about achieving high levels of labour and capital productivity at a company level. This, however, is an interim conclusion which rests on a consideration of physical efficiency. Any final judgement on management actions must finally rest on an analysis of the implication of those actions for costs of production. The reforms in work practices, like the introduction of new technology and the less well-publicised policy of mass sacking were all undertaken with the ultimate aim of reducing costs of production. If these initiatives did not deliver physical efficiency, to what extent did they deliver the desired result of lower production costs?

This question can only be answered on the basis of an understanding of the economics of the car business. As background, Table

2.4 gives two breakdowns of the cost of manufacturing a typical medium-sized saloon in British car factories in 1975. The cost breakdowns are taken from Central Policy Review Staff (1975) and are the best available source on the economics of building cars using the traditional labour-intensive methods favoured by all the British manufacturers, including Austin Rover, in this period. This is the 'base camp' from which the company started before it went for new technology on the Metro line. Tables 2.4(a) and 4(b) show a very similar over all picture. The external costs of bought-out components and materials account for just over half the total cost of building a motor car in Britain in the mid-1970s. Internally controlled manufacturing costs account for the rest. These internally controlled costs can be divided into two main categories, fixed overhead costs of various kinds and variable labour costs. The ratio between fixed costs and variable labour costs is approximately 2:1. Fixed overhead costs account for around 30 per cent of total costs; the first cost breakdown shows fixed overhead costs as 27 per cent of the total and the second, which includes an explicit allocation for the capital cost of new model development, shows fixed overhead costs as 31 per cent of the total. Variable labour costs account for around 14 per cent of total costs. This is the cost of blue-collar, hourly-paid, direct and indirect (production and maintenance) workers employed inside the car factory. On this kind of cost breakdown, the white-collar salaries of line managers, engineering staff, marketing managers, and so on, are treated as part of the fixed overhead cost on the grounds that these white-collar salaries must be paid as long as the firm stays in business, regardless of output levels.

The largest item in total cost is bought-out components and materials, which must have been a promising source of advantage for any car company seeking cost reductions and quality improvements. The Japanese motor manufacturers understood this point well. However, the Austin Rover management was less constructive in its approach to the problem of the company's relation to its suppliers. In a predatory way, they switched contracts and imposed a four-year price freeze on a national components-supplying sector which, by Austin Rover's own calculations, was not achieving productivity increases (Bessant, 1984, pp. 58–68). At the same time, the Edwardes strategy of establishing a smaller Austin Rover, together with Ford and Vauxhall's sourcing decisions, were in equal measure making life very difficult for British component makers in this period. British car output has slumped by 50 per cent since its peak of nearly two million vehicles in the early 1970s. In a

Table 2.4 Breakdown of costs of producing two medium-sized saloon cars in UK factories, 1975

(a) Medium saloon costing £1,100		
Total cost	£	(%)
(i) bought-out components and materials	600	55
(ii) internally controlled costs	500	45
Internally controlled costs		
(i) fixed overhead costs	298	27
(ii) variable labour costs	155	14
(iii) residual	47	4
Fixed overhead costs		
(i) body and assembly factory overhead	145	13
(ii) power train factory overhead	53	5
(iii) tooling	12	1
(iv) engineering	32	3
(v) advertising, sales and administration	56	5
Variable labour costs		
(i) body and assembly labour	113	10
(ii) power train labour	42	4
Residual		
(i) freight	19	2
(ii) warranty	28	3

(b) Medium saloon costing £1,150[1]		
Total cost	£	(%)
(i) bought-out components and materials	600	52
(ii) internally controlled costs	550	48
Internally controlled costs		
(i) fixed overhead costs	360	31
(ii) variable labour costs	155	13
(iii) residual	35	3
Fixed overhead costs		
(i) operating overhead	260	23
(ii) capital overheads	100	9
Variable labour costs		
(i) assembly labour	87	8
(ii) power train labour	42	4
(iii) stamping labour	26	2
Residual		
(i) warranty	35	3

Source: Central Policy Review Staff (1975, pp. 75, 93)

1. The main difference in this second example is that it includes an explicit allocation for the capital cost of model development with a development cost of £72 million spread over 90,000 units a year.

supplying industry which was losing scale, Austin Rover's predatory policies weakened its suppliers without safeguarding supplies of cheap components. In 1983, Austin Rover bought approximately 85 per cent of its components in Britain and argued that it was paying a price premium of at least £24 million over what the same components would cost if the company bought them in continental Europe (Bessant, 1984, p. 62). On this basis, the unconstructive relation to component suppliers was costing the company a penalty of around £60 per car. The failure to control component cost and quality was clearly a major lost opportunity.

If hourly labour costs accounted for around 14 per cent of the cost of building a motor car, this cost category hardly seems the obvious starting point for a car manufacturer seeking cost advantage. On the other hand, it could be argued that although bought-out components were the most important item and a major potential source of advantage, the problem is that these costs were externally controlled. A management like Austin Rover's, which wanted quick results, was likely to prefer an attack on internally-controlled costs which were clearly within its own sphere of influence. In cars in the mid-1970s, direct and indirect hourly labour costs accounted for no more than one-third of these internally controlled costs. But the problem with the remaining two-thirds of internal costs was that they were fixed, which means simply that they could not easily be avoided in the short run without closing the business. In a multi-plant operation, the Edwardes team had, and used, the option of closing peripheral plants, but many fixed costs could not be avoided. From this point of view, although variable labour costs accounted for under one-sixth of the cost of building a motor car, labour-cost reduction was likely to figure prominently in any calculation of cost advantage. By a process of elimination, when it was difficult to control or adjust other (larger) cost items, cost-cutting management was bound to privilege labour costs. In this respect, the Edwardes team was behaving reasonably because the first responsibility of the management strategist is to choose objectives which are within the realm of the possible. But the second responsibility of the management strategist is not to exaggerate the benefits which the enterprise will achieve by attaining its objectives. And here BL management deluded itself. Throughout the struggles with the work-force in the early 1980s it was implied that work-practice reform and low pay settlements were crucial to the control of variable labour costs and it was also implied that the control of labour costs by these means was crucial to securing the financial future of the company. As we shall now argue, there is reason to doubt both these presumptions.

When Michael Edwardes took over, the company did have a labour-cost problem and a major saving in labour cost was then achieved by the policy of massively reducing the labour force. Given that the strategy was to aim for a smaller car company, the policy of widespread shedding of labour was necessary. In the late 1970s, unit labour costs must have been a problem because the company's car output had declined by nearly a half while the size of the cars work-force had stayed much the same. Back-of-envelope arithmetic shows the necessity for the sackings; when the company was carrying twice as many workers as it had needed to build each car in the early 1970s, variable labour costs must have been near 30 per cent of total costs of production. It is also easy to show that the savings obtained were massive. Consider, for example, the benefits at Longbridge where nearly 10,000 workers, or just over half the work-force, was dismissed in the early 1980s (*Financial Times*, 17 June 1982). At the then current rates of pay, each dismissal saved the company about £9,000 per annum in wages, social insurance and pension. The total saving was thus around £90 million per annum which was spread over the plant's early-1980s output of around 275,000 cars a year (170,000 Metros, 50,000 Acclaims and 50,000 Minis). This represented a reduction in unit labour costs of around £325 a car. The saving was huge in a company which could not long have survived if it had retained the surplus workers and the extra labour cost.

At the same time, it must be emphasised that the policy of mass redundancy was essentially a defensive one which normalised labour costs by reducing them to their standard 15 per cent and could do little more. As we have already noted, the Edwardes team did no better than bring the overall size of the Austin Rover work-force (blue collar and white collar together) into line with the reduced output of the cars division. The new management team of the early 1980s was not restrained by union resistance or any squeamishness about removing workers and it would no doubt have liked to do better. But the scope for such a policy was limited by the composition of the work-force; of the 42,000 people employed at Austin Rover in 1984, some 14,000 (33 per cent) were managerial and clerical (*Financial Times*, 22 November 1984) and under the new automated production systems up to a further 8,000 (19 per cent) may have been indirect manual workers providing maintenance and other services. Thus, perhaps half the 1984 work-force was not directly engaged in production, and most of these workers had to be retained as long as the company stayed in business, whatever the level of production. The negative strategy of wholesale sacking encounters natural limits which ensure that it cannot in itself generate a 'productivity miracle' or transform production costs.

When the policy of mass sacking had reached its limits, the incremental gains from the imposition of reformed work practices were inevitably small. Reformed work practices could only save some part of the normal hourly labour cost of 15 per cent. We have already mentioned the complication of indirect (maintenance and service) labour which, because of new technology, accounted for an increasing proportion of the labour force, even though maintenance labour was deployed on a 'multi-skill' basis with few of the old craft demarcations surviving. Equally important is the point that reformed work practices and new technology only saved labour time in some processes. For example, when the Metro was planned, the company calculated that power train production at Longbridge would account for 25 per cent of all labour hours and it did not envisage any reduction in the labour input in those processes. On the Metro, the prime savings were in body and assembly labour costs which (including stamping and all indirect labour) accounted for just 10 per cent of the total cost of building a car in both the CPRS cost breakdowns. If the company was committed to a struggle to claw back some part of 10 per cent of total costs, this looks like much ado about nothing; given the economics of the car business, the reform of work practices could only save a tiny proportion of total costs.

At this stage, it is possible to define the nature of the company's miscalculation about the reform of work practices. Austin Rover has made disingenuous claims about improved efficiency and we have devoted some space to demonstrating that reform of work practices did not transform efficiency and could not transform profitability. The argument so far does not necessarily imply that the company should not have tried to reform work practices; the management view, which it would be difficult to challenge on the information available, was that work-practice reform was essential because it would not have been possible to build cars efficiently with 1980s technology if 1970s work practices had survived. If this view is correct, work-practice reform was a necessary condition for efficient low-cost production. But work practice reform was never sufficient in itself to deliver these desirable objectives, whose attainment depended on two supplementary conditions; the company would have to make an appropriate choice of new technology and be able to sell the output which the factories made. These supplementary conditions will be analysed in the next two chapters, where we will argue that neither of the supplementary conditions was satisfied. Put another way, the problem was management's confusion about strategic priorities. Michael Edwardes and his managers behaved as though the labour problem was *the* strategic problem which had to be solved because the work-force was the major obstacle to high levels of capital utilisation on new equipment which was otherwise inherently productive. However, in any enterprise, the benefits from a reform of work practices (and new equipment) will only be significant if management has an overall strategy which is sensible in relation to the market outside the firm. Where, because of market limitations, any company has difficulty in selling its product, the physical output gains from the reform of work practices and new equipment may be negligible. As Chapter 4 will argue, market limitations were a pressing problem at Austin Rover. In effect, therefore, the post-1977 strategy was unreasonably preoccupied with the work-force who were (at worst) the minor internal obstacle to productive continuous full utilisation of the company's production facilities. It neglected the major external constraints in the market-place outside the factory which would remain when the work-force had been reduced to compliance and docility.

If we are interested in the causes of this miscalculation, what has to be explained is the discrepancy between tactical shrewdness and strategic inadequacy. Under Michael Edwardes, the company's tactics in the struggle with its work-force were quite outstanding in that management obtained every single one of its major objectives without making concessions and without provoking any serious stoppage in the car factories. But purposive tactics were deployed within the framework of a strategy which was crippled because the priority of different objectives was either not examined, or was incorrectly resolved. In part, the miscalculation was predetermined by Sir Michael Edwardes's personal style and by the way in which the company was organised. Sir Michael's own belief, forcefully expressed in his autobiography, was that the task of management was 'to regain control of the company'. Characteristically, the charge against his predecessors was simply that 'management lost the will to manage'. These views were not forcibly challenged because Sir Michael reorganised the company in a way which ensured that the priority of the labour problem was likely to be reasserted rather than cooly and critically appraised.

Sir Michael had strong views about the form of organisation which was appropriate in all large enterprises; such organisations should be decentralised and the head office should be kept small. This was the organisational formula which he had developed when he was chief executive at Chloride and there it worked to transform profitability in the short run. The winning formula was re-employed at BL. The centralised car manufacturing operation which Ryder had created was broken up and the firm 'reintroduced the marques' which were to operate on a stand-alone divisional basis. Michael Edwardes also refused to work from BL's large corporate headquarters in London and created a new small head office which finally employed no more than 200. In this model of corporate organisation the chief executive's responsibility is to select competent divisional management, delegate authority to them, and then back them up. From this point of view, it is understandable that considerable emphasis was placed on the psychological testing of senior management; selection procedures are potentially of great importance in this kind of organisation. It is also significant that Edwardes was scathing in his criticism of earlier BL top managers for failing to back up their divisional managers. Throughout the autobiography, there is a tendency to disparage the staff function and to show a strong preference for line managers; one of the problems of Ryder's BL, it was asserted, was 'too many staff men in line jobs'. One consequence was to diminish the staff input into the decision-making of senior management; decision and initiative were located at the divisional level. The Edwardes philosophy was that it was not part of corporate head office's role to 'second guess' these decisions. It was in this context that the labour problem was privileged. There can be no doubt that senior divisional managers and line managers at every level were preoccupied with the labour problem. They were close to the problem inside the factories and it was time-consuming; in the old order, some line managers had spent half their time trying to solve labour problems. Under the principle of mutuality, many of them had suffered substantial indignity at the hands of the work-force. Within the organisation which Sir Michael created it is easy to see how the labour problem became privileged. One result, as the next chapter will show, is that too little attention was given to the needs as well as the opportunities presented by the new technology.

3 / Investment Strategy

The inquiries into the British car industry and BL in the 1970s placed varying emphasis on the importance of underinvestment and the legacy of a long period of low investment. The Central Policy Review Staff report was impressed by the importance of bad work practices and concluded firmly that 'inadequate capital equipment is only a minor cause of low productivity' (Central Policy Review Staff, 1975, p. 87). But the House of Commons Expenditure Committee was impressed by the evidence that fixed assets per man were generally lower in the British car industry than in continental Europe and BL was particularly disadvantaged in these terms (Table 3.1). On the basis of this evidence, the House of Commons Expenditure Committee (1974–5) report argued that, although work practices might be a problem, labour productivity could not rise to competitive levels as long as the British worker had less equipment at his elbow than his continental counterpart. The Ryder report into BLMC endorsed this verdict and added the point that the quality of plant at BL was inferior because it was much older than the plant in the factories of every other major European manufacturer (Ryder, 1975, p. 20). The implication was that capital productivity also could not rise until new investment was undertaken.

Table 3.1. Fixed assets per man, 1972

Company	Assets per man (£s)	Company	Assets per man (£s)
GM (US)	4,346	Saab	3,141
Ford (US)	5,602	Renault	2,396
Opel	3,612	Ford (UK)	2,657
Daimler	2,694	Chrysler (UK)	1,456
Volvo	4,662	Vauxhall	1,356
Ford (FRG)	3,608	Fiat	3,160
Volkswagen	3,632	BLMC	920

Source: House of Commons Expenditure Committee (1974–5, Table 14).

All this was taken on board in the strategy that Ryder formulated. The *de facto* nationalisation of the car company in 1975 provided an opportunity for a new start with the state supplying the investment funds which BMC/BLMC had never generated from the business of making volume cars in the 1960s and 1970s. The emphasis on the problem of underinvestment was again carried through into the Edwardes plans after 1977; the new management team planned a smaller car company but did not doubt the necessity for a massive investment programme. Along with new product and reform of work practices, investment in new process technology was always a major objective in the recovery strategy.

It has already been emphasised that reform of work practices was necessary because the company was introducing new technology. The relation between investment in new product and in new process technology was less direct. A new range of products could not have been introduced without substantial expenditure on retooling the factories; much of the equipment inside the car factories was, and is, model-specific and has to be scrapped whenever new models are introduced. But the company planned and carried through an altogether more ambitious programme of modernisation in the central assembly plants which Michael Edwardes described as Dickensian. At least £500 million was spent on this purpose. Expenditure was high because state funds were made available at a point in time when there had been what an Austin manager described as 'a radical breakthrough in the application of advanced technology to the (car) manufacturing process' (Butler, 1981, p. 41). In a complex multi-process manufacturing business, the impact of new technology is always uneven. The major changes in the technology of car manufacture in the later 1970s were concentrated in the process of car body building which turns stamped panels into painted shells ready for trim and final assembly. In European factories the necessary welding and painting operations had traditionally been carried out by operatives with welding and spray guns; but, by the mid-1970s, almost all these operatives could be displaced by some combination of jig multi-welders, automatic body framing machines and robot welders and sprayers.

Austin Rover's factory modernisation programme centred on the installation of one automatic body line in each of its two central plants. The first of these lines was installed at Longbridge to build the Metro small car from 1980 onwards; on this line over 80 per cent of resistance welds were applied automatically. The scale of the operation is indicated by the company's expenditure of £106 million on the line and by the size of the new body shop which was built to accommodate the line; the 'New West Works' contained over a million square feet of factory space. A second automated body line was installed at Cowley to build the Maestro and Montego models from 1983 onwards. This second line was a more high-technology facility because it extended the range of operations undertaken by robots on and off the body welding lines; for the first time in a European factory, robots were used to install the front windscreen of a car. More than one hundred robots were installed and the company announced that its aim was to be, by 1990, 'one of the most intensively robotised motor manufacturers anywhere in the world' (*Auto Engineer*, April–May 1984, p. 56). The new hardware on the automated body lines could not be worked efficiently without the back-up of sophisticated computerised manufacturing control systems. Austin Rover was a pioneer in this field and its managing director of operations described the resulting production process as a 'single, totally integrated, computer-based, engineering system' (*Auto Engineer*, April–May 1984, p. 56).

After Ford and the Model T, car manufacturing became a classic large-scale, mass production business. Capital-intensive automated techniques always produced a cheaper product but because the machines were expensive and inflexible, this kind of automation was the prerogative of large-scale producers who could rely on a high process throughput of identical models. Thus in the 1950s and 1960s, automated body building was technically feasible with the aid of jig multi-welders which were 'dedicated' or model-specific so that they had to be scrapped when the model was changed. In Europe, such equipment could only be profitably used to build complete bodies by VW, which uniquely produced one model (the Beetle) in large volume for nearly thirty years. But the changes in production technology in the late 1970s made a new generation of automated body building equipment accessible to all the other European producers, who made a variety of models in shorter runs. The change of technological paradigm is epitomised by the increasing use of flexible robots which are not model-specific. The robot is a device which can be programmed (and reprogrammed) to discriminate the differently shaped panels used in different models and model variants; within its arc of movement, the robot will then execute whatever welding operations are necessary. The European prototype for new-style flexible automated body building is the Fiat Robogate System which can build three variants on each of two different body shells, in any desired mix, up to a total of 225,000 units each year. This new facility was under construction when Austin Rover planned its first body line to build 325,000 Metros a year at Longbridge and was in operation when the company laid out its second line to build 270,000 Maestros and Montegos a year at Cowley.

The new generation of automated equipment is available to all volume car producers. In so far as large-scale producers have lost the advantage which their monopoly of automation once conferred, the economics of the cars business have changed. Some academics have argued more radically that new technology has transformed the prospects of smaller car firms:

> In the late 1970s the introduction of computer controlled production lines plus the introduction of much more flexible automation involving robots, automated handling, machining cells, etc., have changed the economies of scale in production drastically. The use of robots instead of dedicated multiwelders, for instance, gives these plants a greater degree of flexibility to switch models in response to demand and reduces the cost of introducing new models and variants . . . . The major consequence of these advances in production technology has been to reduce the economies of scale in production, thereby reducing the pressure for a minimum output of two million units. A full range of cars can now be produced in one or two plants at a much lower total volume and at a cost which is competitive with much larger producers. There is no doubt that this has been the biggest factor that changes the fortunes of smaller and medium sized producers (Jones, 1985a, pp. 151–2).

On this view, the message of the new flexible technology is that small-scale car producers can now hope to survive and make profits in a way in which they could not in an earlier period of inflexible, dedicated automation where large-scale producers had all the productive advantages.

If this is so, it is certainly good news for Austin Rover. As a result of market failure and the deliberate post-1977 decision to create a smaller company with a capacity of around 750,000 cars, Austin Rover is, in volume terms, the poor relation of the full-line, high-volume European car business, especially as its actual output in the first half of the 1980s was generally below 400,000. As Table 3.2 shows, the major European volume car producers have production volumes of 1.2 million to 1.8 million cars per year; that is, the European majors make three to five times as many cars per year as Austin Rover. Table 3.2 also shows that market position aggravates Austin Rover's problems. Specialists like Volvo or BMW have a similar output to Austin Rover but these firms are not selling volume cars at down-market prices and they do not have to produce a full

Table 3.2. Production volume of European, American and Japanese car firms, 1984 (thousands)

Low volume		Medium volume		High volume	
Daimler Benz	442	Chrysler	1,204	GM	6,450
BMW	367	Honda	970	Ford	3,890
Suzuki	351	Mazda	668	Toyota	2,317
Volvo	265	Mitsubishi	521	VW	1,881
Alfa-Romeo	197	BL	391	Nissan	1,771
Isuzu	133			Fiat	1,415
Saab	90			Renault	1,287
				Peugeot/Citroen	1,232

Source: SMMT, *Annual Statistics*, 1984.

Table 3.3. Model volume at Austin Rover

	1982	1983	1984
Metro	174	175	145
Maestro	2	102	81
Montego	—	—	59
Acclaim	58	50	32
Mini	52	49	35
Rover SD1	33	34	—

line of four models (small, light, medium, large). Austin Rover occupies a uniquely unfavourable position in the European cars business as a small-scale producer of volume cars for the mass market.

In this situation Austin Rover is necessarily producing a range of models which must all sell in relatively low volume. As Table 3.3 shows, Austin Rover's output of around 400,000 cars is spread over six models. The company's best seller is the Metro, whose production volume dropped to 145,000 in 1984, when Maestro and Montego were jointly being produced in similar volume. But, as Table 3.4 shows, this kind of model volume is low by European standards, when European best sellers are being made in volumes of between 300,000 and 500,000 cars per annum. The basic point is that Austin Rover's small and light cars sell at around half the volume of their continental competitors. Several European firms, like Mercedes and Volvo, make and sell specialist large cars in greater volumes than Austin Rover achieves on its mass market small car.

The European majors are, therefore, making individual models

Table 3.4. Production volumes of the ten European best-selling cars, 1984 (thousands)

VW Golf/Jetta	733
Fiat Uno	482
Ford Escort	425
GM Kadett/Astra	389
Renault 11	380
Peugeot 205	375
Ford Fiesta	368
GM Ascona/Cavalier	329
Renault 9	328
Renault 5	304

Source: Automative Industry Data (in *Financial Times*, 2 May 1985).

like the Golf, Escort or Uno in quantities which are roughly equal to Austin Rover's total output. In the era of Fordist mass production, a relative scale disadvantage of this sort would have been quite disastrous for any company which could not find a specialist niche in the market. But, according to senior managers at Austin Rover, in the era of new technology, the relatively small scale of the company is no longer an insuperable handicap. In a radio programme in the spring of 1986, the company's director of operations, Andy Barr, claimed, new technology 'is most certainly giving us a future . . . Most of the pundits have fondly told us over the years that you had to produce something like over two million cars to be efficient. We don't recognise that as being true any longer because the technology that we have adopted in this company has made virtually a lie of that' (Andy Barr, 'File on Four', Radio 4, March 1986).

From this point of view, investment in new technology was not simply a cost necessary to the creation of a more productive car company, such investment also provided an opportunity to redress the balance of productive advantage which had traditionally favoured larger car companies. This position must raise questions about the extent to which the benefits of flexibility were available to smaller car manufacturers and the extent to which Austin Rover captured those benefits through its investment strategy. But, before we turn to examine these questions, we will first consider the more traditional issues about the amount of capital investment at Austin Rover and the return on that investment in physical and financial terms.

If any enterprise embarks on a strategy of capital-intensive automation, then the amount of capital per worker will increase as the strategy is executed. A successful outcome in physical efficiency

Table 3.5. Gross assets[1] per man employed in Austin Rover, Ford UK and BMW, 1984

ARG	£14,260
BMW[2]	£12,277
Ford (UK)	£15,843

Source: Austin Rover, Ford and BMW Annual Reports.

1. Gross assets equals plant and machinery excluding land and buildings.
2. BMW figure is for 1983.

terms would be indicated by a rise in capital productivity, that is, the amount of capital used to produce each unit of output should decline, because the firm is obtaining an increase in productive output which is proportionately greater than the increase in capital input. If gross assets per employed worker are the measure, there can be no doubt that Austin Rover's investment strategy did raise the level of capital input to levels which now compare favourably with those obtained by other European car firms. As Table 3.5 shows, the capital equipment gap which existed in the mid 1970s had been closed by the mid 1980s; by 1984 Austin Rover's gross assets per man were no longer markedly inferior to those of Ford UK, which had itself invested heavily in new technology in the early 1980s, and Austin Rover actually had more assets per worker than the specialist BMW which had a comparable-sized output.

It is more difficult to judge capital productivity. When Austin Rover was making extravagant claims about labour productivity, it was significant that the company was completely silent about capital productivity. The published accounts do not allow us to construct a series on capital productivity for Austin Rover Group since 1977, because of corporate reorganisation. The best we can get is a series which runs from 1977 to 1981 for BL cars (which includes Jaguar and Triumph as well as Austin Rover), and then from 1982 onwards is limited to the Austin Rover Group. The effect of this is simply to understate the points we wish to make. If it were possible to take the sums attributable to Jaguar and Triumph out of the earlier figures, our points would emerge much more forcibly. Even as it is, however, real gross assets per employee more than doubled between 1977 and 1984. More specifically, Table 3.6 summarises the productivity results of this increase in capital intensity, using again the measure of gross assets per unit of output. As can be seen, the capital productivity performance was distinctly inferior. At constant 1980 prices, the gross assets employed to produce each unit of output increased from £975.60 to £1,222.50 between 1977 and 1984 even

Table 3.6. Gross assets employed per unit of output at BL (at 1980 prices)[1]

	Gross fixed assets[2] (£m)	Production in units	Assets employed per unit of output (£)	Index	Gross assets employed per unit of output (1980 money values) (£)
1977	519.9	741,138	701.5	71.9	975.6
1978	527.2	714,738	737.6	79.1	932.5
1979	641.8	598,236	1,072.8	88.2	1,216.4
1980	742.1	501,499	1,479.8	100.0	1,479.8
1981	777.9	479,896	1,621.0	103.3	1,569.2
1982	606.6	390,834	1,552.1	109.9	1,412.3
1983	554.7	458,330	1,210.3	117.2	1,032.6
1984	595.7	390,130	1,526.9	124.9	1,222.5

Source: BL Cars Reports and Accounts, 1977 to 1984.

1. BL Cars from 1977 to 1981 (including Triumph and Jaguar) and Austin Rover Group thereafter
2. Gross assets are plant and equipment at cost minus disposals plus additions during the year.

after allowing for the fall in the series resulting from the privatisation of Jaguar cars. As explained previously, the increase in this ratio implies a proportionate decline in capital productivity over this period. Put still more starkly, what this table demonstrates is that by the simplest relevant physical measure the programme of investment in new technology failed.

If we are interested in explaining this failure, the first point to emphasise is that capital productivity was poor because of low process throughput; the new equipment is not working at anything like full capacity at either plant or line level. The company closed the peripheral Rover Triumph plants at Speke, Solihull and Canley, thereby reducing capacity by some 250,000 (see Bhaskar, 1979). But this did not solve the problem of overcapacity because the two remaining central assembly plants at Longbridge and Cowley had a standard two shift capacity of at least 750,000 and that was much more than the company needed in the late 1970s and early 1980s.

The capacity to build this number of cars was the result of deliberate decision by the post-1977 management since both Longbridge and Cowley were re-equipped during this period. Capacity in the central plants was hardly reduced at all when the two automated body lines were installed. At Longbridge, the Metro body line in New West Works had a design capacity of 6,500 built-up cars and 1,000 knocked-down kits each week (Willman, 1984, p. 194). This, indeed, understates the position. A substantially larger output of 400,000 built-up Metros per annum can be obtained from these facilities; Harold Musgrave has claimed 'if we really wanted to have a go these days we could produce up to 8,000 cars per week from the New West Works' (Robson, 1983, p. 186). At Cowley, the configuration of the facilities is such that it is harder to define the capacity of the Maestro–Montego line. But throughput is immediately limited by the capacity of the equipment in the weld and paint processes through which all the cars going down the line must pass; we know the pre-treatment and priming process has a design capacity of seventy-two cars per hour (*The Engineer*, 19 April 1984) and this translates into an annual two-shift capacity of 288,000 cars per annum. So, the company's two new high-volume lines at Longbridge and Cowley have a joint capacity of nearly 700,000 cars per annum and the two central plants could build more cars than this because the company has maintained separate low-volume lines which build cars like the Mini and Rover 213.

At a line level, the new automated body building lines represent a £250 million investment in overcapacity which must inevitably compromise the physical productivity of the new capital equipment. Ironically this dilemma is most acute on the much-vaunted Metro line which must operate at significantly below the 50 per cent capacity utilisation attained on the Maestro–Montego line. In the New West Works at Longbridge the company laid out two parallel lines for building Metro bodies; each line was separately fitted out with all the machines necessary to turn Metro panels into finished painted bodies. Austin Rover planned to carry out trim and final assembly on several lines in both Car Assembly Buildings 1 and 2. One of the two body lines in New West Works was *never* used in the first four years of production (Willman and Winch, 1985, p. 144). Final assembly facilities were also underutilised because the company initially used only two out of three assembly tracks laid out in CAB 1 (Robson, 1983). As a result, capital utilisation on the new Metro facility is almost as bad as in the worst recorded case in the old BMC/BLMC company. The all-new Cofton Hackett engine plant, originally built in the late 1960s to provide overhead cam E-series engines for the Maxi had a capacity utilisation of no better than 36 per cent in its first ten years of production (Hartley, 1981). With a capacity of 400,000 cars per year and maximum production of around 170,000 cars per year, the Metro facility had a capacity utilisation of no better than 43 per cent in its first five years of production. With this kind of utilisation of the capital equipment, the company's achievements on the lines which were being used becomes entirely irrelevant.

The new kind of automated body lines may require less throughput than the old kind of dedicated lines but two of them have the capacity to produce much more output than the company needs and neither of them can therefore be worked efficiently. After successful reform of work practices in the early 1980s, it is no longer possible to blame or scapegoat the workers for low output levels on the new facilities. Indeed the results concerning deteriorating capital productivity simply confirm the conclusions drawn from our examination of work-practice reform in the last chapter: even if work-practice reform was a necessary condition for improvements in physical efficiency, it was not a sufficient condition. Process throughput is low (and capital productivity inferior) because, as the next chapter will show, market limitations ensure that the company cannot sell anything like the 750,000 cars which the company could make each year. The failure of the investment strategy in nationalised cars shows that, just as in nationalised steel, sophisticated capital equipment is not inherently productive if the enterprise cannot sell its output (Williams *et al.*, 1986). In physical terms, the company has rectified a problem of underinvestment only to produce a new problem of pathological overinvestment; the company's factories contain large amounts of expensive, recently bought capital equipment which is not being used productively and cannot be used productively as long as the market will not absorb the full output from that equipment. This point is of more than academic interest because overcapacity and underutilisation create pressing financial problems for the enterprise.

Investment in New Technology: the Justification

New technology in the 1980s usually involves the substitution of capital for labour, and this was certainly so on the new Austin Rover body lines. It is incorrect to suppose that the men were all directly replaced by robots. As Table 3.7 shows, on standard two-shift working, one robot in a car factory only replaces two manual operatives. But the labour saving from a combination of robots with other automated equipment on Austin's new body lines was really

Table 3.7. Number of men replaced by one robot

	One shift	Two shifts	Three shifts
Assembly and handling	0.3 – 1.0	0.6 – 2.0	1.0 – 3.0
Spot welding	0.7 – 0.9	1.5 – 1.75	2.1 – 2.5
Arc welding	0.5 – 0.75	1.0 – 1.5	1.5 – 2.2

Source: Hartley (1985, p. 36)

Table 3.8. A comparison of direct manpower in traditional and automated body building

Operation	Traditional methods: men per shift	Metro (automated): men per shift
Body side assembly	58	10
Dash lower assembly	5	1
Underframe floor assembly	76	11

Source: Butler (1981, p. 46).

dramatic. As Table 3.8 shows, some operations on the Metro line at Longbridge required just one direct worker where six had been employed before. Employers usually introduce this kind of new technology because it reduces total manufacturing costs when the extra cost of the capital equipment is more than covered by a large saving in labour costs. But this was not the case with automated body building, where Austin Rover's own calculations showed that traditional labour-intensive methods of building were cheaper. A 1976 company document shows how labour and capital inputs varied in different body building techniques (Table 3.9). Labour and capital costs for a conventional 1970s 'gateline' body building system are taken as a base of 100 and the labour and capital inputs of alternative body building methods are related to this base; as the table shows, the Metro body building system took out two-thirds of the labour at the expense of adding 75 per cent to the capital input required. No published document discloses the cost base on which such percentage reductions and increases operated. But the company had this information and concluded that 'automated options were generally found to be more expensive than conventional' (Willman and Winch, 1985, p. 190); even with the benefit of engineering assumptions about efficient usage of full capacity, 'the

Table 3.9. Labour and capital inputs with different body building techniques

Build method	Labour input	Tooling and equipment input	Typical application
Conventional gateline	100	100	Marina, Maxi, Princess
Box jig	151	129	Longbridge Mini
Intermittent build	143	152	
ABF (Unimate)	34	176	Metro 1 ADO 88
Intermittent Eurobuck	68	176	Ford

Source: Willman and Winch (1985, p. 57).

company could not make the overall cost of using the high technology look cheaper' (Willman and Winch, 1985, p. 50). In strict cost terms, the company's investment in automated body building was economically irrational.

Automated body building did, however, offer other benefits which were decisive for the company. Like other car manufacturers, Austin Rover chose automated body building because it offered higher build quality. Car body shells have become increasingly highly engineered structures over the past fifteen years. Structural integrity is required to ensure collision safety while weight saving is at the same time required to reduce manufacturing costs and improve economy and performance. The design team's brief is to produce a lighter, stronger (and ideally more durable) body shell. This kind of shell can most easily be manufactured in volume on a modern automatic body line. Automatic lines offer predictable weld quality and that is obviously important in structurally critical areas of a highly engineered shell. Such lines also offer much higher standards of dimensional accuracy. On a manual body line with poor quality control body frame variances will be a constant problem; an ABF line should work continuously within tolerances of a couple of millimetres. This accuracy is important in a variety of ways. On the Maestro and Montego for example, the windscreen is glued into the body shell as a way of strengthening the structure; this operation requires a windscreen aperture which is dimensionally accurate. The imperatives of the business are such that all volume manufacturers have to install automatic body lines.

There were also more company-specific motives which derived from the managerial obsession with the labour problem at Austin Rover. When new technology was perceived as an instrument of labour control, the displacement of labour became almost an end in itself. As Willman and Winch observe, 'there were felt to be unquestionable advantages in using a technology which resulted in management having to deal with fewer operatives'; specifically this would 'make it easier to achieve targets about volume, quality and continuity of output' on the Metro line (Willman and Winch, 1985, p. 50). Automatic technology was attractive partly because it could discipline a hitherto recalcitrant work-force. In the new order, the direct work-force was much smaller and production was organised so that the remaining direct work-force was constrained to work steadily; most of these direct workers were employed on pick and place jobs feeding the automatic machines at the pace of the machines. The main Metro body line was laid out so that each direct worker had to perform one repetitive operation over a short time cycle (Table 3.10). By way of comparison, on the original Mini line in 1959, no production operation had a cycle time of less than the standard 144 seconds. In this new management utopia, car body building would become like food processing (biscuit-making and bottling) where everything moves smoothly at a pace determined by the automatic machines.

Table 3.10. Machine cycle times on the Metro body line (seconds)

Loading sub-assembly robot	20
Loading underframe multi-welder	50
Pick-up welding	100
Body framing line	96
Body apparatus lines	120

Source: Willman and Winch (1985, p. 15).

In some ways, the Metro facility could have been seen as the line manager's revenge, but the strategy of automation was a risky one because if things went wrong (as they did) and the new lines were not fully utilised, then the work-pace would become more relaxed and the expensive new equipment would create problems concerning high fixed costs. Many workers in the Metro body shop cannot be driven hard because management has extended machine cycle times to prevent 'overproduction'; the ABF equipment, for example, which was planned to run on a cycle time of forty-five seconds was, in spring 1986, running on a cycle time of three minutes (works visit). More seriously, underutilisation of such equipment created a fixed-cost problem which was threatening because survival in the car business depends on the management of fixed costs. The CPRS cost breakdowns for 1975 show that, with traditional labour-intensive build methods, fixed costs were twice as large as variable labour costs and accounted for 30 per cent of the total cost of the car. Factory overhead costs are a major component in total fixed costs and factory overhead can only be controlled by achieving a high level of capacity utilisation.

Under the recovery programme the company tried to control factory overhead costs by a policy of closing peripheral plants and concentrating production in the two central assembly plants. As we have already noted, the Rover and Triumph factories at Speke, Solihull and Coventry, along with Austin Rover's Belgian assembly plant at Seneffe, were all closed between 1980 and 1982 while Longbridge and Cowley were being re-equipped. Michael Edwardes was quite explicit about the rationale for these closures, 'the only way to reduce fixed costs substantially is to close actual factories' (House of Commons Expenditure Committee, 1981, Q. 151). The closure of peripheral plants removed a substantial fixed-cost burden. Two of the closed plants. Speke and Solihull, were themselves substantially underutilised and operating well below break-even point: Speke had a capacity of around 100,000 cars but production never topped 30,000 cars per year (Bhaskar, 1979, chap. 7); Solihull, which had a two-shift capacity of 3,000 cars and a break-even of 2,000 cars per week, was producing 1,000 cars a week when it closed (*Sunday Times*, 17 May 1982). However, the benefits which the central factories obtained from the closure of the peripheral factories were inevitably limited when the Rover and Triumph factories were producing specialist cars in low volume. There was no high-volume throughput which could be transferred to the central plants and very little throughput was transferred. A central part of the new management strategy was to concentrate on a compact model range, so all the Rover and Triumph models (except for the SDI hatchback) were discontinued when the peripheral factories closed. The closure of the Belgian assembly plant looked more attractive in production engineering terms; Seneffe had been assembling 50,000 or more Minis and Allegros from British kits and this throughput could be sent down the underutilised Longbridge lines. But, as the next chapter will explain, this decision was disastrous in marketing terms because it undermined Austin's volume sales in Belgium which were based on the company's status as an indigenous assembler.

If the throughput benefit from peripheral closure was small and capacity was not reduced when new technology was installed, the company's two central plants remained underutilised and their fixed costs were so high that the company could not make a profit at the output levels which it achieved or could realistically hope to achieve. Senior company sources (*Financial Times*, 12 January 1985) have recently explained how Longbridge and Cowley need to be loaded with throughput if the company is to make a profit. After a major cost-cutting exercise, Longbridge and Cowley cannot break even at a trading level without covering depreciation if throughput falls below 435,000 cars. A volume of around 650,000 cars is required if the company is to earn sufficient profit to cover depreciation and finance new investment (without any interest payment on already invested capital). As the company has a capacity of around 750,000, then the Austin Rover situation is not so different from that of the mass car producers who need capacity utilisation of 70–80 per cent before they break even after covering depreciation. On the company's own calculations a capacity utilisation of 87 per cent (a volume of 650,000 cars) is necessary if the company is to earn the profit to finance new investment. Since 1980, production has never bettered 475,000 and averages 423,000; in the past six years, therefore, capacity utilisation averages just 56 per cent. Eighty per cent capacity utilisation will never be achieved when the company has 200,000 surplus capacity at Longbridge in the form of dedicated lines which, as we will argue later, can be used to build Metros and cannot be used to build anything else. In the unlikely event that all the other lines at Longbridge and Cowley worked at full capacity, the company would achieve no better than 73 per cent capacity utilisation. Equally an output of 650,000 cars per annum cannot be achieved because of the market limitations which will be analysed in the next chapter. The company had ambitious plans to raise output to 535,000 cars in 1985 and 575,000 cars in 1986. These plans were simply unrealistic and an expansion of output in the first six months of 1985 produced stocks of unsaleable cars which were being remaindered in later 1985 and early 1986.

At this point it is possible to sum up the financial predicament which the company was in after massive investment in new technology. Capacity underutilisation on the new lines pushed up fixed costs to the extent that the company could never make a profit. On the labour costs side, through new technology and work-practice reform, the company may have saved part of the 10 per cent of total costs. But, on a broader view, there were no net savings in cost as new technology was introduced; for, as Austin Rover chipped away at variable labour costs, its fixed costs were increasingly out of control. This was a problem which Michael Edwardes had identified when he took over the company in 1977; he told the House of Commons Expenditure Committee, 'you start with a high fixed cost and you do not start with the potential or the capability of producing the vehicles to cover that cost' (House of Commons Expenditure Committee, 1981, Q. 151). Ironically, this statement can be said fairly to describe the predicament of the company when Michael Edwardes left it in 1982 after massive investment in new technology. The argument, however, does not end here. We must recognise that, in this respect, Austin Rover's position was no worse than that of many other European car companies which cannot make profits out of underutilised new technology. In this situation, new technology might still be worthwhile for Austin Rover if the balance of competitive advantage between the company and its larger European competitors had shifted when the industry made the investment in new technology.

The New Technology: Possibilities and Limitations

There is disagreement about whether and how the traditional economies of scale in car manufacture have been affected by the introduction of new technology. Senior industry figures, like Bill Haydon of Ford, firmly reject the claims of Austin Rover's managers: 'Austin Rover have to convince their shareholders, which happens to be the British public, and so they get carried away with their utterances . . . Economies of scale aren't operating under different rules. I think that is a myth' (Bill Haydon, 'File on Four', March 1986). On the other hand, academics like Altshuler and Jones, who collaborated on the MIT International Automobile Program looking into 'the future of the automobile' came to quite a different conclusion: 'a producer with modest volume in several individual (product) lines can (now) offer these at a competitive cost, whereas until recently it appeared that a medium sized or specialist producer's volume could support competition only on the basis of unique product attributes since costs would be high' (Altshuler, *et al.*, 1984, p. 182).

Significantly the MIT team failed to provide any statistical back-up for their claims. Various estimates of minimum efficient scale in different processes have been cited in the literature on the industry until recently (see, for example, OECD, 1983, p. 72) but all these estimates date from the 1970s before new technology was introduced. The academics who now claim that scale economies have diminished rest their case on the observation that the new techniques of automated body building are more flexible and therefore accessible to small producers. But clearly it is illegitimate to leap from this observation about one process to the conclusion that the economics of the business have changed fundamentally. As industry figures like Haydon point out, the cost of developing new models is still very high. It is also true that the process throughput requirement (outside body building) remains high. A review of the evidence on these points suggests that powerful economies of scale still favour the larger producer with larger model runs.

New model development was cheap in the Porsche–Issigonis era when cars could be designed by one man and prototypes were built in a shed behind the factory. But, from the mid-1960s, new models were increasingly 'cost-engineered' in a world which imposed ever more complex safety and emissions requirements. New model development itself became a large-scale activity requiring extended teams of specialists supported by expensive hardware and sophisticated software. With CAD simulation, a car company can go back to the computer rather than back to the drawing board or back to the workshop. That controls the manpower requirement but it does not make new model development cheap. Ford demonstrates this point by calculating the 'renewal cost' of introducing new models (which includes the costs of development plus necesary factory retooling). A typical European major, marketing a full line of five or six models would expect to introduce one new model each year if it was operating on a five-year model life. On Ford's estimate, this car company faces a 'renewal cost' of around £500 million each year (company communication, 7 April 1986). The Ford company has certainly spent this kind of money on recently introduced models; the introduction of the Sierra in 1982 cost the company $1,200 million (company communication, 7 April 1986). If renewal costs are so high, in the volume car business they can only be recouped by selling a large number of units of a given model and this is clearly a source of advantage to the larger manufacturer with the longer model runs.

The evidence on process throughput requirement is more ambiguous and contradictory, but none of it suggests that economies of scale have been suspended with the introduction of new technology. In engine production, final assembly is increasingly robotised as on the Fiat Fully Integrated Robotised Engine (FIRE) line. But engine lines are still dedicated to the production of one engine type for a long period at a volume of 300,000 units or more. In Europe, volume car engine production must therefore be the natural monopoly of the major producers who would manufacture two or three families of engines at a volume of 300,000 units each. Furthermore, the extent of the new flexibility in automated body building should not be exaggerated. The new lines can produce a differentiated output of between 200,000 and 350,000 shells for two models and several variants on those models from the manufacturer's current range. But body line equipment is not sufficiently flexible to be cheaply and easily reusable when the company changes models every five years or so. For example, most robots in car factories are task-specific in that they can only cope with the geometry of one model or set of models after an expensive process of customisation which includes construction of special purpose fixtures and tools. A recent calculation breaks down the typical cost of building a robot assembly system (Table 3.11). On this basis, if the robot is task-specific, 65 per cent of the original cost of the system is lost when the original model (or models) is discontinued and substantial costs will have to be incurred if the equipment is then to be reused. The small-scale producers may buy such a line of robots but when it comes to using and reusing this line, the large-scale producer with long model runs retains his advantage.

It would be wrong to claim that economies of scale survive unchanged in their traditional form, but substantial scale economies persist in the new technological order. The cars business is not moving towards minimum economic orders of one or twenty-five or 25,000 for radically different models. The future of styling kit manufacturers is secure; those who want a certain kind of individuality will still have to produce a semblance of it by dressing up mass produced models. But the future of Austin Rover can hardly be so secure because, as long as model development costs are large and process throughput requirement remains high, the European major

Table 3.11. Breakdown of cost of a robot assembly system (per cent)

Robot equipment	35
Other proprietory hardware	15
Design, construction and commissioning	50

Source: Flexible Automation Systems (1984, p. 1)

producers with volumes of 1.2 or 1.8 million units per annum retain considerable scale advantages.

The position is unlikely to change with the further development of new technology because the available capital equipment and standard plant layouts reflect the requirements of larger manufacturers who dominate the world car industry. All the car manufacturers in the world use similar capital equipment made or licensed from a few, mainly American and West German, suppliers like Cincinnati, ASEA and Kuka. Tie-ups with equipment suppliers ensure that large manufacturers get first choice of new equipment. Most of the standard equipment is designed to work at high volume, producing 175,000 to 350,000 units per annum, and is most easily used flexibly by large-volume manufacturers. Austin Rover could not order an 'off the shelf' body line with throughput of 350,000 and capacity to handle six different basic models and two variants on each model. No doubt such a line is now technically feasible but the equipment-supplying industry hardly has much incentive to develop it when the world industry is dominated by larger manufactures with different requirements. Of course, resourceful plant layout can be used to compensate for the inflexibility of standard equipment. But, here again, Austin Rover is disadvantaged because the larger firms generally have a superior production engineering capability and the financial resources to cover the risks if innovation fails. It is not accidental that the major firm of Fiat constructed the first flexible European body line in the late 1970s when Austin Rover installed an inflexible dedicated line for Metro production. The Metro line at that time simply imitated an earlier paradigm of automated body building developed by GM in its Lordstown, Ohio, plant in the early 1970s. The two small Swedish firms of Saab and Volvo do have a record of imaginative and innovative plant lay-out. But these firms have the cushion of large profit margins on luxury cars; in 1985, after the launch of the 9000 in North America, Saab had a total output of just 100,000 cars but Saab's management claimed the company made a 'clear profit' of £1,000 on each car sold (*Financial Times*, 10 June 1985). Austin Rover is in an entirely different situation when it comes to carrying the costs and risks of innovation.

Our conclusions about the continuing importance of the economies of scale in the new technology car business are confirmed if we examine what small car firms do. Small firms usually buy in major mechanicals. Even with the benefit of cheap labour, new entrants into the cars business must buy in their engines and gearboxes; Hyundai in Korea and Proton in Malaysia provide useful extra volume for Mitsubishi of Japan by buying in engines and gearboxes from that firm. Small West European firms have bought in mechanicals for some time and are now beginning to share the development costs of new body shells. Volvo pioneered co-op deals on engines by buying in a low-volume V6 which Peugeot and Renault also use, while the engines for small Volvos like the 340 have been supplied by Renault. Saab could not afford to develop a new body shell for the 9000 and shared the cost with three Italian manufacturers (Fiat, Lancia and Alfa) who will all produce variant versions of the same shell. Austin Rover executives may say that the economics of the business are now more favourable to small firms but what they do is exactly the same as any other small manufacturer trying to survive in an unfavourable economic environment where scale is important. From 1989 onwards, all the current Austin Rover range will be replaced with new models whose body shells will be 'jointly developed' with Honda. Austin Rover does plan to develop one new engine; £250 million has been allocated for the new K series engine which will be fitted to the company's volume small cars. But two other 'families' of engines and all the company's gearboxes and transaxles will be bought in or manufactured under licence (*Financial Times*, 4 May 1985).

From the scale point of view, the company's strategy of creating a small-volume car firm with an output of around 750,000 cars was certainly a very risky strategy, perhaps even an impossible one. Even if the strategy had been executed brilliantly, the scale advantages in car manufacture were such that the strategy took Austin Rover into the valley of the shadow of death as a car manufacturer. Any European firm making 750,000 volume cars a year must live with the ever-present threat of being relegated from manufacture to assembly of another manufacturer's kits. When Michael Edwardes took over in 1977, he found that Austin Rover was negotiating a collaboration deal with Renault. He personally vetoed this on the grounds that the logical outcome of collaboration would be the subordination of Austin Rover as Renault's junior partner; 'BL would become no more than an offshore assembly operation' (Edwardes, 1983, p. 194), and the main benefits would have accrued to Renault who, as he rightly emphasised, would have gained access to Austin's British dealer network. But if the particular deal with Renault was deemed inappropriate, other collaborative arrangements were still desirable and the company looked round for a more suitable partner. The choice eventually fell on the Japanese firm of Honda, whose car output was not so different from that of Austin

Rover; as late as 1984, after rapid expansion, Honda made less than a million cars. But, when Honda could use the profits from world leadership in motor-bike production to finance a systematic development of car manufacture, Austin Rover was inevitably the weaker partner in the relationship, the one which would find it difficult to escape relegation to assembler status. It is likely that Honda at the end of the 1980s will now obtain the advantages which were denied Renault at the end of the 1970s.

There is no simple invariant trade-off between small size and inability to survive as an independent car manufacturer. The smallest European car manufacturer, Saab, has survived against all odds by deliberately moving up-market into the manufacture of sporting and luxury cars which find a highly profitable niche in the United States market. However, the economics of the business are such that, after the failure of the post-1977 recovery strategy and with output well short of the planned volume of 750,000, Austin Rover is now too small to survive as an independent manufacturer of volume cars. At this end of the market, when Austin Rover's recent total output averages 450,000, then the burden of high model renewal costs spread over low volume is sufficient to kill the possibility of profit. Consider, for example, the case of the Metro, whose development cost the company £275 million; some £106 million was spent on the body shop in New West Works and the rest was the development and tooling cost for an all-new body shell (Willman and Winch, 1985, p. 44). The West Works body shop is dedicated and, if the automated equipment is to be used, can build nothing except Metros. In this case the whole £275 million should be written off over the life of the model. The company will keep the Metro in production for some eight years. But, since the Metro is a reskin of elderly mechanicals and the European small car business is highly competitive, it would be prudent to write off the development cost over a five-year period. The company planned to make 350,000 Metros per annum, a model volume that is quite respectable in European terms. On this scenario each car would carry a development charge of £157 (£275 million divided by 350,000 units x 5 years). But the company has never produced more than 175,000 Metros each year or half as many as it planned. This volume shortfall means each Metro carries a development charge of £314. Since the Metro is a small cheap car, this kind of extra development charge attributable to low volume must kill all the profit.

As a small-scale producer, Austin Rover now faces in acute form the traditional cost problems which have handicapped British car manufacture. The 1975 CPRS Report into the problems of the British car industry showed that the industry's most important cost problems stemmed from low volume which imposed a cost penalty because the substantial fixed costs of developing new models had to be spread over a small output during the life of the model. Firms like Ford, Vauxhall and Talbot have solved this problem by annexing their British plants to the European manufacturing and assembly strategies of their multinational parents. This outcome reflects the discretionary sourcing decisions of multinationals who have concentrated their manufacturing operations in continental European plants. At Austin Rover a similar outcome is now increasingly overdetermined by the ineluctable economics of the car business; with output stuck around 450,000 after the failure of the post-1977 strategy, Austin Rover no longer has the volume base to sustain independent manufacture of motor cars. It was always Utopian to believe that new technology would change the size of the minimum necessary volume base in car manufacturing. When it did not and the market would not absorb anything like 750,000 cars, Austin Rover seemed unlikely to have a future as an independent manufacturer.

Flexibility for What?

New technology could not redress the balance of productive disadvantage for small-scale producers. But for a company which hoped to stay in the game as a manufacturer of 750,000 cars per annum, automation and new technology were a necessary defensive response. From this point of view, the quality of the company's decisions about automation did matter. Good decisions on new technology would at least have minimised the company's disadvantages and would have allowed Austin Rover to defend manufacturing more effectively or at least manage an orderly retreat into assembly from a position of relative strength rather than desperate weakness. In the event, poor decisions on new technology compromised the company's capacity to adapt to the failure of the strategy when the new models (especially the Metro) sold in much lower volume than the company had planned. Automation could and should have been used to deliver a kind of flexibility which was an insurance policy against this kind of outcome. Austin Rover's failure to capture the relevant benefits of flexible automation has never been analysed. It is obscured by the romantic nature of much of the literature on new technology. There is a strong tendency to assume that such technology automatically delivers 'flexibility' and that this flexibility is a kind of undifferentiated technological benefit which is pursued and captured in the same way by all the producers in the industry.

In the cars business, as in most others, flexibility is not a simple universal technological imperative. With the new technology automated flexibility comes in several different forms. When different enterprises have different strategies for obtaining competitive advantage, it is unlikely that all the enterprises in the business will pursue the same form of flexibility with the same degree of urgency. This is so because productive flexibility is not an end in itself but an instrument which is, or should be, used and adjusted in a way that is determined by the firm's broader market and financial calculations. To be more specific, it is useful to distinguish between 'marketing flexibility' and 'product-mix flexibility'. These are two quite distinct concepts of flexibility which enterprises pursue for different strategic reasons. 'Marketing flexibility' is a productive capability required so that the enterprise can implement a marketing policy of stimulating differentiated consumer demand. The driving force is a Japanese-style marketing philosophy which emphasises rapid model change from one generation to the next plus the proliferation of models and derivatives so that the current generation of product occupies every niche in the market. An enterprise with this marketing philosophy requires factories which are flexible in the specific sense that they can in each generation produce the broadest possible range (of models and variants) before changing over as cheaply and easily as possible to the next generation of models. 'Product-mix flexibility' is a different kind of productive capability which is required as a way of adjusting to unpredictable variation in the composition of consumer demand for a given range of models. Depending on the market, the product range can be broad or narrow and the enterprise makes no deliberate attempt to broaden the range. The driving force here is the production engineering problem that arises when firms have to meet demand by producing a range of models in proportions which are unpredictable and may shift during the life of one generation of product; if build lines are dedicated to one model the firm is likely to find that some lines are underutilised while others cannot produce the output that is required. An enterprise with this kind of problem requires factories which are flexible in the sense that they can turn out a variable model mix.

When the basic distinction between marketing flexibility and product-mix flexibility has been established, it is easy to demonstrate that, because car manufacturers have different strategies, some firms pursue marketing flexibility while others pursue product-mix flexibility. Different enterprises thus exploit new technology in different ways. Marketing flexibility is an important objective for the larger Japanese manufacturers who are committed to broad product ranges and short model lives. But it is much less relevant to European manufacturers. The West German manufacturers, like VW, BMW and Mercedes, who lead the European industry, all have an austere marketing philosophy of narrow product range, few variants and model lives of between five and seven years with little face-lifting. It is instructive to compare the ranges which Nissan and VW currently sell on the British market(Table 3.12). Nissan claims 5 per cent of the British market with a range of no less than 10 models which includes two sports coupés, a tall car and a four-wheel drive utility vehicle. VW claims a similar share with a range of six models and two of these (Scirrocco and Audi 80 coupé) are sports coupés which share floorpans and major mechanicals with the company's volume-selling light and medium cars. Since their marketing philosophies are so different, West German and Japanese manufacturers exploit the potential of automation in a different way. The showpiece of European high-technology is VW's Hall 54 at Wolfsburg, where 25 per cent of Golf and Jetta final assembly is automated and robots are used for such tasks as battery installation and clipping brake lines to the underfloor. With a long run of one unchanged product, VW is able to design the Golf around the capability of the automated equipment. And to simplify matters further, the specialist firm of Karmann assembles the Scirrocco coupé variant of the Golf. At Nissan, management's approach to automation is consciously and explicitly different; here automation has to be adapted to the company's need to produce different models (for example, the Micra and Sunny) on a single line before carrying out model change-overs with minimum retooling every three years (*Industrial Robot*, December 1984, p. 252).

Flexibility of this sort is not required by most European firms who choose a 'harder' kind of automation. The European firms have thus pursued product-mix flexibility on their new body lines and many of them can now send two different models down the same line. The European norm in this respect can be established by briefly describing the mass production body facility which Ford has built at Dagenham and the specialist production facility which BMW has built at Munich.

Table 3.12. Nissan and VW model ranges

Nissan Model	Class	VW Model	Class
Micra	small	Polo/Derby	small
Cherry	light	Golf/Jetta }[1]	light
Sunny }[1]	light/medium	Scirrocco }	light coupé
Prairie }	tall	Passat/Audi 80/90 }[1]	medium
Bluebird	medium	Audi 80 Coupé/Quattro }	medium coupé
Laurel	large	Audi 100/200	large
300C	large		
Silvia	sports		
300Z	large sports		
Patral			

Source: *Autocar*, 9 April 1986

1. Bracket indicates models sharing floorpan and major mechanicals.

At Dagenham, the aim was to develop a body line where two entirely different models (currently the Fiesta and Sierra) can be automatically welded on one line (*Industrial Robot*, December 1984, p. 227). The main achievement, however, was in the finishing lines. Up to this stage flexibility involved the capability to handle variants of a particular model with no difficulty and to enable tool changes necessary to shift from one model to another to be handled much more quickly than previously. But at finishing 'the respot line can handle different models . . . The . . . robots can carry up to 64 programmes and it is a simple matter for the robot to recognise which body shell it is about to weld and change its programme accordingly' (*Industrial Robot*, December 1984, p. 227). The benefit is that the production facility can adjust instantaneously to variations in British market demand for Ford's small and medium cars. The sales success of the Fiesta and the relative sales failure of the Sierra does create problems for Ford but at least the company's production engineers have ensured that this pattern of demand can be met in a factory which remains sensibly utilised.

BMW pursues a similar kind of flexibility through the construction of 'mixed lines' that can build bodies for both the 3 and 5 series cars which are the company's two volume-selling models. The most interesting aspect of BMW's manufacturing strategy is that this company has a different approach to the same objective of product-mix flexibility at the finishing stage of body welding. BMW operates a 'cellular' system in finish welding. Each tack-welded body is placed in a spit or turntable and clamped into position. At the same time another vehicle shell is welded up on the bottom face of the turntable. In each cell (of which there are six) there are four robots which carry out the 571 welds in a 4.5 minute cycle time. A sophisticated 'micro-wave' communication system identifies the model variant entering each control station and the robots are appropriately and automatically programmed. This system allows BMW to vary the production mix of 3 and 5 series body shells by feeding in different models to the finishing cells. By adding or subtracting cells, the company can also quickly scale up or down total body building capacity to match fluctuating market demand. For a relatively small manufacturer needing to adjust promptly to the market changes for its relatively expensive product this was an obviously intelligent strategy.

It is in this context that Austin Rover's exploitation of automated flexibility should be judged. Some indicators suggest that the company has the same amount of automation as its competitors; at Longbridge and Cowley, as in other modern car plants, 90 per cent of body welds are applied automatically on the Metro and Maestro–Montego lines. But this automatic equipment delivers less flexibility than in some other European factories and, in relation to the company's strategy, this technology delivers the wrong kind of flexibility. When Austin Rover introduced new technology, the company obtained more marketing flexibility and less product-mix flexibility than its strategy required. Fundamentally, this was because the company failed to integrate the pursuit of flexibility into its broader corporate strategy.

The recovery strategy aimed to create a narrow product range, as Sir Michael Edwardes told the House of Commons Select Committee on Trade and Industry (1981, Q. 188), the strategy was to 'end up with about four model families', one of which would be a Jaguar large saloon. As the development funds were limited, the new 'model families' were small and model lives would be long because rapid change-over was quite impossible. By the time it is discontinued at the end of the 1980s, the Metro will have been in production for eight years and the family will include just two variants (a three-door and a five-door and hatchback). The company's needs for marketing flexibility were therefore exceedingly modest and when the new body lines were constructed, Austin Rover built in more flexibility than it needed in marketing terms. Flexibility to handle model variants was never an important objective on the Metro line at Longbridge partly because the company always envisaged a long model life with just two or three variants being produced; but as a precaution, this line was laid out with spare stations in which the equipment for dealing with variants could be installed at a later date. At Cowley flexibility to handle variants was built in right from the beginning; the automatic body framing station (ABF) included a finished weld track capable of identifying and spot welding up to five different body types. At present this line is only building three variants (Maestro hatchback, Montego saloon, Montego estate) and the company has no plans to introduce more variants.

If Austin Rover has too much marketing flexibility on the Cowley line, more generally the company has much less product-mix flexibility than it needs to meet the varying composition of demand for its narrow range of models. In this respect, the company's new automated facilities are inferior to those of European competitors like Ford or BMW which we have already described. Geography is part of the problem as Austin Rover is a small car company with two separate major assembly plants. Since the Metro line at Longbridge was more than fifty miles away from the Maestro/Montego line at Cowley there could never be any possibility of varying the mix between small and light/medium cars inside one facility, as Ford does at Dagenham. But this geographic constraint was exacerbated by poor decisions about choice of machines at Longbridge and about plant layout at Cowley.

At Longbridge, as the manager of Austin Rover's manufacturing strategies later made clear, management carefully considered the mix of new technology which would be used to build the new Metro. In the body in white (BIW) sub-assembly area, where automatic operations were most fully introduced, the company chose to rely mainly on multi-welders incorporating 'automatic transfers, turnover devices and the latest generation of welding equipment fully supported by solid state control circuitry' (Butler 1981, p. 42). These were supplemented by a very limited number of robots (four Unimate robots used in the material handling mode, two ASEA robots for fusion welding and one Unimate for resistance spot welding). The overall result in the BIW sector, where the body shell is made up from numerous pressings by welding, was that, whilst over 80 per cent of resistance welds were applied automatically, only 9.5 per cent of these were by robots and 70.9 per cent by multi-welder. This choice of machines entailed a loss of product-mix flexibility; when multi-welders predominated, the body line in the New West Works was dedicated in that it could only produce Metros. The result was that Austin Rover had no insurance against the possibility that its new small car might fail to sell in the volume which the company planned. As we will argue in the next chapter, market limitations ensured that the Metro did not sell and, consequently, the Metro facility is substantially underutilised with a capacity of over 350,000 and annual throughput of 175,000 or less. Because the line is dedicated, this underutilisation cannot be eased by sending other Longbridge models (like the Mini or Rover 213) down the line. Rover 213 bodies are now built in the same shop as the Metro, but the building process is entirely separate and does not use any of the automatic machines or the six-and-a-half-mile conveyor system originally installed for Metro body production. The process of building Rover 213 bodies is relatively labour-intensive with 30 per cent of welds made manually, and finished Rover bodies are, at the suggestion of Honda engineers, transported on a new robot trolley system (factory visit, May, 1986). On the Metro line, the company invested more than £100 million in creating inflexible excess capacity which cannot now be used to do anything except build an extra 200,000 Metros that nobody wants to buy.

These mistakes were not repeated at Cowley when the company came to build its second modern body line. From the outset it was recognised that 'the planning for the next generation of cars . . . will require much more flexible facilities' (Butler, 1981, p. 54). Flexibility had to have a high priority on the Maestro–Montego line because the company planned to manufacture two models in the one facility and to introduce more variants than had been the case with the Metro. The machine mix was therefore changed so that robots figured much more prominently; more than one hundred robots were installed and, besides the 'conventional' welding robots, the underframe assembly also used, for the first time in the UK, portal gantry robots. But the new plant was laid out so that the line, which could deliver more model variant flexibility than the company wanted, delivered less product-mix flexibility than the company needed. The inferiority of the Cowley line in this last respect can be established by comparing it with Ford's Dagenham line which has already been identified as a model of European flexibility; this plant layout comparison is a fair one because the Cowley and Dagenham lines were built at much the same time and used many similar machines. Figures 3.1 and 3.2 show that the plant layout for underbody and side panel framing is very similar at Cowley and Dagenham. But from the tag welding process onwards the Cowley layout is different; whereas Ford sends two entirely different models (Fiesta and Sierra) down one line in the later processes, Austin Rover sends two related models (Maestro and Montego) down two separately designated parallel lines with duplicate process equipment dealing separately with the two variants. The resulting difference in product-mix flexibility is considerable. The Ford system, as we have already observed, is designed to cope with variations in the mix of demand for Sierra and Fiesta whereas the Austin Rover system presupposes a fifty-fifty split in demand for Maestros and Montegos. Any deviation from a fifty-fifty split in demand threatens to leave the company with excess capacity on one parallel line and a bottleneck on the other. In 1986, if there had not been excess capacity on both parallel lines, Austin Rover would have been in serious trouble because the Montego was selling twice as many units as the Maestro.

The error of the more romantic literature on new technology is to suppose that this technology contains one simple message of good news for all car manufacturers, especially small ones. If there is one message in the technological battle, it is the old one of 'to them that hath shall be given' because economies of scale are still powerful in the new order. But, more fundamentally, the point is that the potential of new technology is complex and that much depends on how and for what purposes that technology is exploited by enterprises with disparate business strategies. Austin Rover's miscalculation was that it did not sufficiently appreciate this point and therefore invested in high-volume automated facilities which offered very little of the model-mix flexibility which the company needed. When the demand did not materialise in anything like the planned quantity, the fixity of the new capital-intensive way of building cars became a problem; on the Metro line, the company was left with excess capacity in a high fixed cost facility which was then necessarily inefficient and unprofitable. Austin Rover's production engineers must presumably accept responsibility for the poor layout of the Cowley line, but these production engineers cannot be blamed for the worse mistakes over machine choice at Longbridge. The company's production engineers did what they were asked to do. As Willman and Winch observe, 'flexibility was not high on the Metro agenda. The brief given to those purchasing the equipment and ultimately to the project team was in terms of a given volume of a particular car with known characteristics and specified man hours' (Willman and Winch, 1984, p. 52). This point is confirmed by one of the company's production engineers who noted that the company had not chosen 'a fully flexible manufacturing facility' for the Metro because it was assumed that the one model would be produced at

Figure 3.1. Flow diagram illustrating plant layout at Rover Group Cowley for the Maestro and Montego

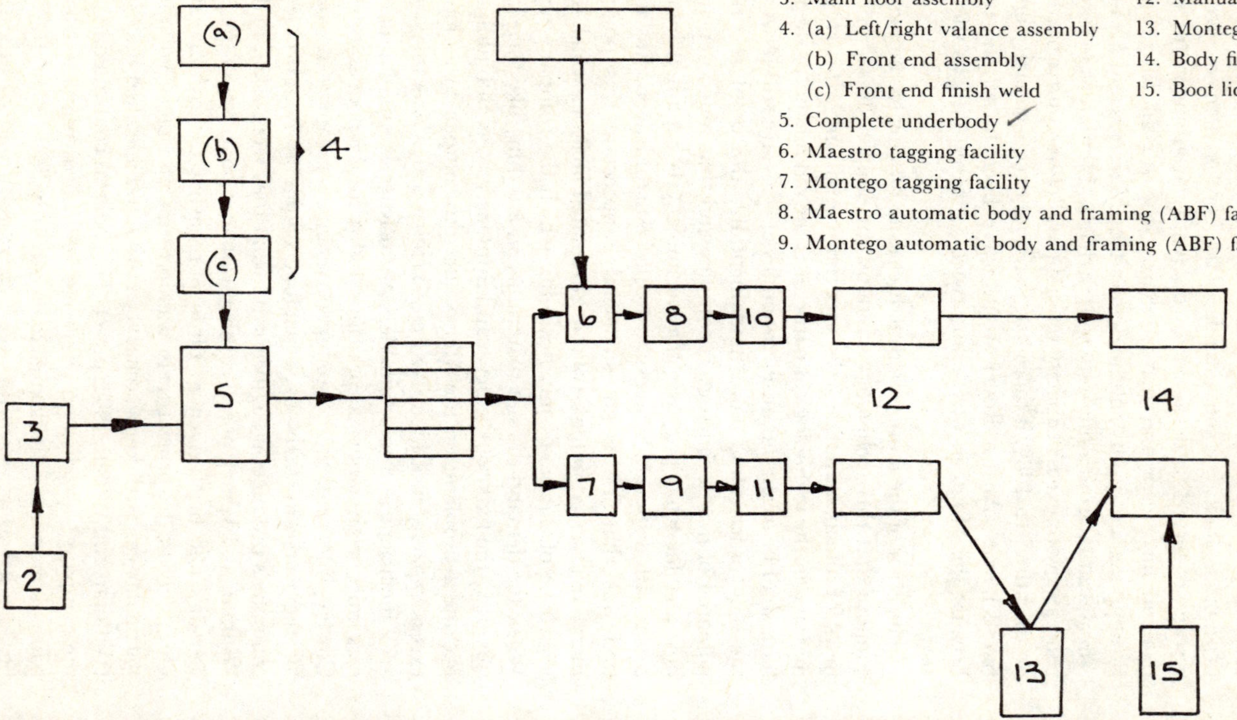

1. Body side assembly
2. Rear end assembly
3. Main floor assembly
4. (a) Left/right valance assembly
   (b) Front end assembly
   (c) Front end finish weld
5. Complete underbody
6. Maestro tagging facility
7. Montego tagging facility
8. Maestro automatic body and framing (ABF) facility
9. Montego automatic body and framing (ABF) facility
10. Maestro finishing weld
11. Montego finishing weld
12. Manual finish weld
13. Montego brazing line
14. Body finishing line
15. Boot lid/doors fitted

Figure 3.2. Flow diagram illustrating plant layout at Ford Dagenham for the Sierra

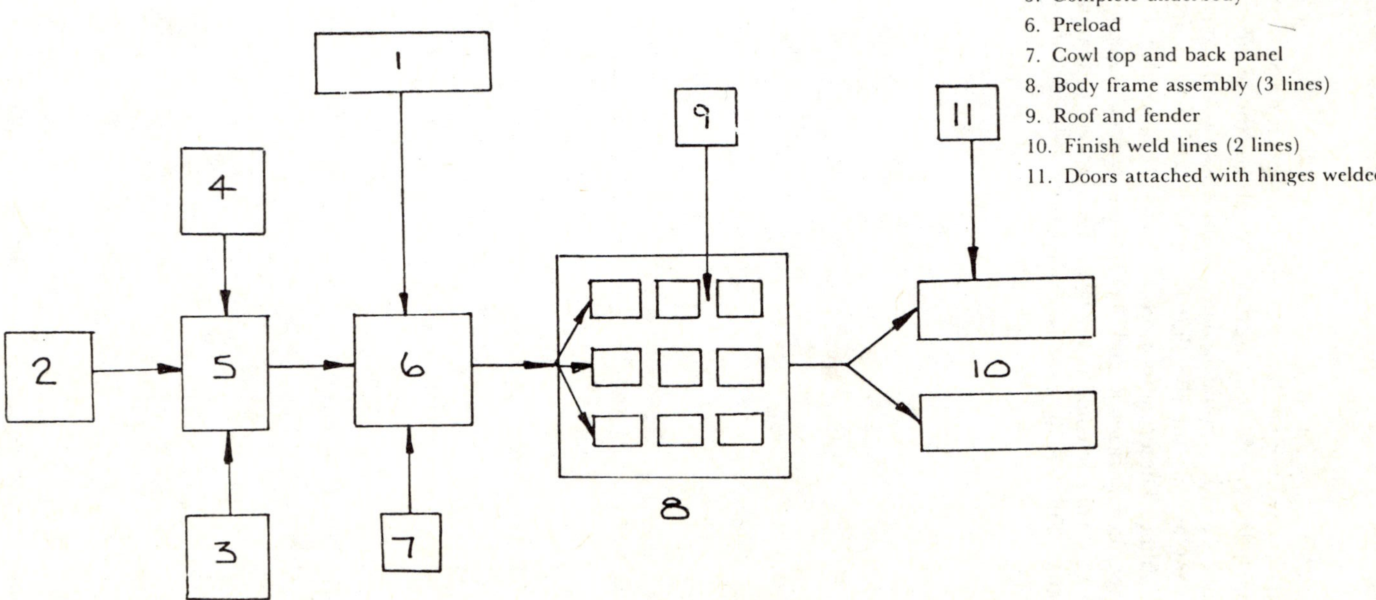

1. Body side assembly
2. Rear underbody assembly
3. Front floor
4. Engine compartment
5. Complete underbody
6. Preload
7. Cowl top and back panel
8. Body frame assembly (3 lines)
9. Roof and fender
10. Finish weld lines (2 lines)
11. Doors attached with hinges welded

high volume for some years (Butler, 1981, p. 45). Senior management gave the production engineers the wrong brief which did not include a 'worst case' scenario for sales or the requirement that the new facilities should be laid out in a way which covered the company against the risk that the new models would not sell in high volume. These points were neglected because senior management accepted unrealistic and overoptimistic sales projections. The projected volume could never be achieved when the company faced the kind of market limitations which are the subject of the next chapter.

4 / Market-Led Failure

This chapter considers the problems posed by the car market in Britain and abroad. The two previous chapters have established that there was a major disjuncture between the strategic priorities of management and the real internal problems of the business; the reform of industrial relations was necessary but did not justify the overriding importance given to it and the commitment to inflexible automation created a new internal problem. Management also represented the problem of low sales at home and abroad as an internal problem; low sales were attributed to the inadequacies of the product range in the late 1970s and that, of course, was an internal problem which management could rectify by developing new models. The product range was a real problem, but this chapter develops the argument that sales were more fundamentally constrained by market limitations; even after the introduction of new models, Austin Rover sales were limited by the composition of demand on the home market and the inadequacy of the company's European distribution network. The implication is that the management was mistaken in supposing that the key problems were inside the company and therefore Austin Rover's future depended on what the company did itself by way of tackling the internal problems of labour productivity, process technology and product range. Even if management had exactly identified and solved all the real internal problems, the productive and financial rewards would still have been limited because the basic problem was outside the company in the market-place.

The market is now a problem for all the European manufacturers who face certain common problems in the 1980s. There is a market for about 10 million new cars each year in Western Europe. But, according to a recent report of DRI Consultants, the industry has the capacity to produce at least 12 million cars per year (*Autocar*, 22 May 1985). The European manufacturing industry is extremely fragmented. There are six major producers each holding about 11 per cent of market. In recent years there has also been a convergence of demand on to Euro-standard motor cars; the majors now have lookalike models competing against each other in each market segment. Each major tries to win extra volume by exporting from its home base into all the near European markets. If these conditions create problems for all the European volume car manufacturers, they hurt some manufacturers worse than others and Austin Rover worst of all.

Under current market conditions, none of the majors can avoid carrying their share of overcapacity, but most of them can still build reasonable model volume through a combination of home and export sales. As Table 4.1 shows, the European majors build the 400,000 plus sales of their best-selling models in a quite stereotyped way; they take sales of 200,000 or more for the model on its home market and then export between 25,000 and 80,000 cars to each of the major European markets. At a company level, this kind of sales success requires a characteristic pattern of representation in different national markets. The ideal pattern for a major is a strong market leader's position with a share of more than 25 per cent in its home market and a position of 3–5 per cent strength in all the other European markets. Strength at home and abroad are to some extent substitutes for each other: Fiat is a relatively weak exporter which relies on holding nearly half its home market, while VW prospers with less than 30 per cent of its home market because it is the strongest intra-European exporter with more than 5 per cent of most of the major markets.

Table 4.1. Sales of the four best-selling European motor cars in the major national markets 1984 (thousands)

	France	Italy	UK	W. Germany	Total
VW Golf	39	60	29	*313*	539
Ford Escort/Orion	23	31	*208*	84	497
Fiat Uno	27	*331*	21	39	451
Renault 9/11	*212*	62	28	28	435

Source: 'Motor Industry Survey', *Financial Times*, 11 September 1985

Current market conditions are particularly threatening for Austin Rover in the 1980s because the company lacks the pattern of market representation necessary for decent model volume. Austin Rover's problem is that, as Table 4.2 shows, it lacks strength at home and abroad. Export volumes fell badly in the late 1970s and levelled out at around 100,000 cars per annum. In the crucial near-European markets, Austin Rover did not have a significant market presence; the company held well under 1 per cent of the mainland European

Table 4.2. Austin Rover production, home sales and exports 1978–85

Year	Production[1] (000s)	Export allocation (000s)	Output exported (%)	UK sales (000s)	Total UK market (000s)	ARG market share[2] (%)
1978	611.6	247.9	40.5	373.8	1,591.9	23.5
1979	503.8	200.2	39.7	337.0	1,716.3	19.6
1980	395.8	157.8	39.9	275.8	1,513.8	18.2
1981	413.4	126.2	30.5	285.1	1,484.7	19.2
1982	383.1	133.9	35.0	277.3	1,555.0	17.8
1983	445.4	118.3	26.6	332.7	1,791.7	18.6
1984	383.3	78.6	20.5	312.1	1,749.7	17.8
1985	465.1	—	—	328.0	1,832.4	17.9

Source: SMMT *Annual Statistics*.

1. Includes Jaguar for all years except 1984 and 1985 (Jaguar production in 1980 was 15,469, rising to 25,467 in 1983) because comparable figures to subtract from exports are not available.
2. Includes Austin Morris, Rover and Triumph, but from 1980 excludes Jaguar (1978–9 figures include some 5,000 or 6,000 Jaguar saloons).

market. In the 1980s, 75 per cent or more of the cars produced by Austin Rover have been sold at home; no mainland European producer is anywhere near as dependent on its home market. And, on this home market, Austin Rover's market share has been stuck below 20 per cent since 1976 and more or less constantly around 18 per cent since 1981; no European major lives with such a low share of its home market. The implications for overall production and individual model volume are considerable; since 1982 the company's normal 18 per cent share of the market produces home sales of between 275,000 and 325,000 which are spread across six Austin Rover models. With export volume and home market share both stuck on a plateau, the main influence on Austin production volumes becomes cyclical variation in the overall size of the British market. As Table 4.2 reflects, a modest revival of production in 1983–5 was largely caused by an upswing in new car registrations from a recession trough of 1.6 million in 1980 and 1981 to around 1.8m in recent years. In a mature market, where there is only a slow secular increase in new registrations, cyclical upswings of demand only offer limited and temporary relief.

If the company's recent history is one of market-led failure, this outcome was not what the Edwardes team planned or anticipated. In the late 1970s, Austin Rover relied on three ageing models (the Mini, Allegro and Marina) in the volume car market; management's premise was that 'the company did not have the models that people wanted to buy' (Willman and Winch, 1985, p. 33). The solution to this problem was to develop three attractive new models (the Metro, Maestro and Montego) which would sell in high volume; management's assumption was that this compact model range could initiate what Michael Edwardes called a 'product-led recovery'. The new models would directly replace the Mini, Allegro and Marina but as the new models were launched the company would also discontinue a variety of older inherited low-volume models (including the Maxi, Dolomite, Princess) which sold at volumes of 50,000 a year or less. This process would be quite painless because the company assumed that the new models would sell in high volume. The company estimated that the Metro, for example, could sell 350,000 cars per annum (Willman and Winch, 1985, p. viii), which implied that this car would be a European best-seller. Edwardes seemed not to doubt that this was possible, and worried only about the problem of 'product gap' (Edwardes, 1983, pp. 173–4); after the first new model (the Metro) was launched in the autumn of 1980, there would be a two-and-a-half year gap before the company was ready to launch the next new model (the Maestro) in spring 1983. It was recognised that there would be market-share difficulties in this period. But in the late 1970s, after Michael Edwardes took over, it was assumed that the company would claim a home market share of 24 per cent when all the new models were on sale (Edwardes, 1983, pp. 59–60). As late as spring 1982, Austin Rover's sales and marketing director maintained that the company's target was 25 per cent of the British market and 200,000 cars a year in Europe; with a favourable exchange rate and uninterrupted production runs at the factory, Trevor Taylor then claimed 'it has to be on' (*Sunday Times*, 21 March 1982).

With all three new models on sale since spring 1984 it is now clear that these sales targets have not been, and probably cannot be, met. The new models have not raised the company's home market share above 18 per cent nor raised export volume above 100,000 cars. The whole scenario of product-led recovery has turned out to be a fantasy because the new models have not sold in the required volume at home or abroad. If we ask why the new models did not sell, the simplest explanation is that the new product was mediocre in terms of design and build quality. And this consideration must figure as part of any more sophisticated explanation.

In design terms, there is no doubt that the new models did represent a major improvement on the company's previous offerings;

anybody who has driven a Montego and a Marina will readily concede that point. And it is creditable that Austin Rover produced new models which were at least competitive with those produced by other car companies which had larger development resources and better mechanical components in their parts bins. But consumers are not sentimental and their verdict is clear: Austin Rover's new products simply are not good enough to compete with the current generation of product from companies like GM and VW. This was probably inevitable when the company never had the resources to do the job properly. Austin Rover could only manage to develop two and half models from its own resources (the hatchback Maestro and booted Montego cannot be counted as two different models since they share a similar floorpan and other panels as well as major mechanicals). There was never any money for the development of all-new power trains which have been one of the keys to GM's success in the European market-place with its new front-wheel drive cars. Traditionally the Austin product had offered effective 'packaging' which maximised interior space for passengers and luggage in relatively small cars. All the new models retained these virtues and the media dutifully hyped the Metro as a car which was six inches longer inside than outside. What was less noticed was that Austin's leadership in this area had depended on its pioneering adoption in the 1960s of the space-saving, transverse-engine front-wheel drive configuration. When all the company's European competitors had adopted this layout by the early 1980s, Austin's 'packaging' advantage was inevitably eroded.

As the success of companies like Volvo shows, conservative (or unimaginative) design can succeed if the product is properly developed and build quality is high. But these conditions are not met at Austin Rover; although the company now has a docile work-force in new automated factories, build quality remains relatively poor. This is serious because reliability sells motor cars; a recent independent survey showed that reliability was the first consideration for 80 per cent of new car buyers. Although the company has improved both fit and finish and mechanical reliability, the new models still compare poorly with the rising industry standard. The summary verdict in the 1984 *Which Car Buying Guide* epitomised the problem: the Metro was described as 'improved, except for reliability', while the Maestro was 'roomy but reliability looks worrying'. The extent of the persisting reliability gap between Austin and its Japanese and European competitors was measured in a 1985 Nissan survey of first-year warranty costs on cars sold in the UK (*Autocar*, 6 November 1985). Austin Rover's warranty costs have been substantially reduced in the past few years but first-year warranty costs still amount to £79 per car. Vauxhall and Ford, Austin's two main rivals on the British market, have warranty costs of £30 and £60 respectively. The Japanese firm of Nissan has a warranty cost of just £10 per car.

By 1985, Austin Rover was so worried by the quality gap that it sought improvements through what became known in the company as 'swat teams'. It was reported that 'all Austin Rover's 260 senior managers have been detached for four weeks on a rota basis. Their brief has been to take cars fresh off the line and pound them round Gaydon (test track) to seek faults and to phone customers and dealers for views on shortcomings' (*Financial Times*, 24 February 1986). At the same time fleet managers were being reassured that Austin Rover's chairman, Harold Musgrove, had personally stripped down a 1.6-litre Montego to trace the faulty component which was causing oil leaks.

The problem of the 'non-price characteristics' of the Austin Rover product was and is a serious handicap but its importance should not be exaggerated. With differentiated consumer products like cars, the volume, character and composition of demand in the market-place is likely to be at least as important in determining the level of sales achieved. Furthermore, a high overall level of demand is not enough if the market is segmented and fragmented in a way which limits the sales which can be achieved by any one supplier. Austin Rover's failure in the British market for cars in the 1970s and 1980s provides a classic example of such problems because, as we will now argue, the composition of demand prevented the enterprise from taking 24 or 25 per cent of the British car market with a compact range of just three models. In principle these external market limitations are more fundamental than the poor quality of the company's product because they would have persisted and limited UK sales even if the company had been given the resources, had sorted out the quality problem and had produced three new models which were relatively good. Before we turn to analyse the distinctive problems of the 1980s, we will first explain how the forms of competition and the composition of demand in the 1970s British car market limited Austin Rover sales.

In the 1960s and early 1970s the pattern was one of indirect competition between two majors (Austin Morris and Ford) who between them accounted for 65 per cent of British sales. At the beginning of this period there was little strong direct competition for sales between manufacturers of volume cars. The minor domestic producers (Rootes-Chrysler and Vauxhall) were never a problem because they were effectively British-based firms which lacked the scale and resources to threaten Austin and Ford. The two majors sold differentiated products into distinct market segments. Ford served the fleet and business market with its medium-sized rear-wheel drive three-box saloons, while BLMC sold small front-wheel drive cars to private buyers. Ford did well out of this stand-off because its market segment was growing and never seriously contested by another manufacturer. BLMC did very badly out of the stand-off because its market segment was shrinking and increasingly fiercely contested by importers who sold to private buyers; by 1974 the private buyer segment accounted for no more than 60 per cent of the market and half of these purchasers were buying imports (Williams et al., 1983, p. 235). The inroads of the importers created increasingly acute problems for BLMC; from 1965 to 1975 foreign-badged and manufactured cars increased their share of the British market from 5 to 30 per cent (Williams et al., 1983, p. 281). This led to increasing market fragmentation at home; the share of the top ten best-sellers declined from 70 per cent of the market in 1965 to 49 per cent in 1975. And BLMC suffered disproportionately because Ford's fleet buyers remained loyal to a British (or at least British-badged) car; by 1974 imports had a mere 4 per cent of the fleet market (Williams et al., 1983, p. 235).

By the early 1970s Austin's dilemma was that it was increasingly squeezed between Ford and the importers and the size of its available home market was rapidly declining. It was not possible for the company to displace the importers on the scale required. In Britain, as in most continental European countries, foreign-badged cars have taken one-third or more of the market for the past decade. That result is guaranteed by differentiated consumer demand and is not much affected by the strength of the indigenous major suppliers. By the early 1970s, Austin's only strategic option at home was to beat Ford by breaking into the fleet market. This was the rationale behind the development of the Marina, a conventional medium-sized rear-wheel drive motor car which would sell against Ford's Escort and Cortina. As we have argued elsewhere, the Marina failed to do this job in the mid-1970s (Williams et al., 1983, p. 240). Ford's dominance of the UK fleet market was never challenged by the Marina; thanks to fleet sales, the Ford Cortina (later replaced by the Sierra) and Escort held the number one and two positions in the UK sales charts all the way from 1972 to 1983.

The new team, therefore, faced the old problem of virtual exclusion from the company car market in the early 1980s. In some ways the situation was by this time more open because Ford's Cortina replacement, the Sierra, lacked the market appeal of its predecessor. But Ford's weakness created no big opportunity for Austin Rover, whose task at this time was made more difficult by Vauxhall's advance into the fleet market. This advance was backed by competent product and strong distribution so that the Cavalier, by the mid-1980s, regularly outsold every other model in the fleet market. In 1984, Austin Rover launched the Montego, a medium-sized saloon which (just like the earlier Marina) aimed to win the company a substantial slice of the fleet market. As Table 4.3 shows, it is now clear that this objective has once again eluded the company. Official figures show that the new Montego has not raised Austin Rover's share of the company car market above the 16–19 per cent level which the company held in 1980–4. In 1985 the company did no better in the company car market with the new Montego than it did in 1981 when it was selling the Ital, which was a revamp of the ten-year old Marina model. According to Austin Rover's own estimates, the company in 1985 held no more than 15–17 per cent of fleets with more than twenty-five cars (*Financial Times*, 24 February 1986). Part of the problem arose from an Austin dealer network which was ill-adapted to fleet business because it was still geared up to making private sales. Only after the launch of the Montego in 1984, did Austin Rover begin to develop a network of 125 specialist fleet dealers, but by February 1985 only seventy dealers had been signed up (*Financial Times*, 18 February 1985). One year later, 100 dealers had been signed up and the company then announced that the new network would be 'formally launched in the next two to three months' (*Financial Times*, 24 February 1986).

Austin Rover's static home market share and low sales after 1980 are therefore an indication that market limitations in their traditional form continue to constrain Austin Rover. The company

Table 4.3. Austin Rover's share of the company car[1] market (per cent)

1980	15.9
1981	18.8
1982	16.8
1983	16.8
1984	17.5
1985	19.2

Source: DTI
[1]Company cars are cars registered in company names.

survives precariously by relying on a domestic private market customer base which transfers its loyalty from one generation of BL product to the next. This conclusion is strongly suggested by the way in which new Austin Rover models kill off volume sales of their predecessors when the older model is maintained in production and also by the way in which new models end up selling in roughly similar volume to their predecessors. The old Mini, for example, was being produced at a rate of 200,000 per annum from 1975 to 1978. Volume sales of the Mini were killed off by the Metro after autumn 1980. By 1982 Austin Rover made just 52,000 Minis and 174,000 Metros which left the company more or less where it had been in terms of small car sales in the late 1970s. Again this represents the continuation of an old pattern; for fifteen years or more Austin Rover has been quite unable to make 'conquest sales' at the expense of other marques. *Plus ça change, plus c'est la même chose.*

Although these 'traditional' market limitations continued to operate, they were not the central problem by the 1980s. Indeed, it would be wrong to attribute the failure of the company's strategy to these traditional constraints. By the early 1980s, there was a decisive change in the form of competition which intensified the pressure on Austin's market share. It is these new forms of competition in the car market which are crucial to the recent market failure because under current market conditions it becomes more or less impossible for the company to take 20 per cent plus of the market with three models. In the conditions of the first half of the 1970s, it was possible to suppose that the company might improve home market share if its new models were technically excellent and its distribution network was overhauled. Under the new forms of competition, the company could not improve market share even if these conditions were satisfied.

The most obvious recent change in the British car market has been the emergence of a third domestic major, Vauxhall, which has come back from the dead and aims to take 20 per cent of home market sales with the aid of GM's American financial resources and Opel's design teams and factories (*Financial Times*, 20 March 1986). The majors still sell around 60 per cent of the market but that volume is now split three ways between Austin Rover, Ford and Vauxhall. As Table 4.4 shows, Vauxhall increased its UK market share from 8.2 per cent in 1979 to 16.6 per cent in 1985. From our point of view, the important point is that the resurrection of Vauxhall intensifies the pressure of increasingly severe direct competition between the majors. The era of stand-off and indirect

Table 4.4. Major company shares of UK new car registrations, 1979–85

	Austin[1]	Ford	Vauxhall
1979	19.6	28.3	8.2
1980	17.8	30.7	8.8
1981	18.8	30.9	8.6
1982	17.8	30.5	11.7
1983	18.2	28.9	14.6
1984	17.8	27.8	16.1
1985	17.9	26.5	16.6

Source: SMMT

1. Includes Austin, Morris, Rover and Triumph. 1979 also includes some 6,000 Jaguar saloons.

Table 4.5. Directly competing models from the three majors

Small class	Ford Fiesta Austin Metro Vauxhall Nova
Light class	Ford Escort/Orion Austin Maestro Vauxhall Astra
Medium class	Ford Sierra Austin Montego Vauxhall Cavalier

competition ended in 1977 when Ford entered the small car segment for the first time with the Fiesta, and BL decided to compete for volume sales with new models in all three major market segments. The era of full-line direct competition opened in 1983–4 when Vauxhall entered the small car class with the Nova, and Austin Rover launched its third new model, the Montego, into the medium class. There is no volume market for large cars in Britain; three market classes (small, light and medium) together account for 85 per cent of new car sales in Britain. In each class, the majors now have three similarly-packaged models which have been carefully product-planned to win sales by attracting every available private and business customer. Table 4.5 shows the line-up of directly competing models from the majors.

Direct competition has also intensified because while the majors slog it out toe to toe, the minors can no longer be ignored. The minors are now importers (VW, Nissan, Volvo, Renault, and so on) who typically each claim only 2.5–5 per cent of the market. The im-

Table 4.6. Market shares of the ten best-selling cars in the UK, 1985 (per cent)

		Class[1]	Share
1	Ford Escort	L	8.5
2	Vauxhall Cavalier	M	7.3
3	Ford Fiesta	S	6.8
4	Austin Metro	S	6.5
5	Ford Sierra	M	5.5
6	Vauxhall Astra	L	4.2
7	Austin Montego	M	4.0
8	Ford Orion	L	3.6
9	Vauxhall Nova	S	3.3
10	Austin Maestro	L	3.1

Source: SMMT, *Annual Statistics*.

1. L = light; M = medium; S = small.

porters can use strength elsewhere to sustain a presence in the market with one or two models which are close substitutes for the offerings from the majors. The pressure of competing models from the three majors more or less excludes the importers from the top ten places in the sales chart, but foreign-badged cars now dominate positions 10 to 20 in the sales charts.

The shift from indirect to direct full-line competition is important because it has major implications for Austin Rover. To begin with, the new pattern of competition reduces the volume which can be obtained on the British market with one model in any market class. In the old days of indirect competition, it was possible for a major to produce a class-dominating best-seller which took 10 per cent or more of the total market. Ford was the main beneficiary in the 1970s because it produced the leading model in two classes; in the period 1970–80 the Cortina averaged a 10.1 per cent market share and the Escort, which could claim 9–10 per cent of the market in a good year, averaged 8 per cent. In the era of direct competition, it is rapidly becoming impossible to achieve this kind of market penetration with one model. It is instructive to examine Table 4.6 which shows the top ten UK best-sellers of 1985. This is the first year in which each major has had a fully competitive model on sale in each class for the full year. The pressure of direct competition is indicated by the way in which this table is dominated by the offerings of the three majors who, for the first time since 1976, took all the top ten places and did so with variants of their nine basic models.

From Table 4.6 it is clear that the sales which would once have been made by a class-dominating best-seller, or divided between two majors, are now being split between three best-sellers from different majors. Consider, for example, the medium class, which was long dominated by the Cortina. The Cavalier has been a runaway success in this class, but took only 7.3 per cent of the market against the 5.5 per cent share retained by the Sierra for Ford. In its first full year the Montego was third in this class and took 4 per cent of the market. Just two years previously in 1983, before the Montego was launched, the Sierra and Cavalier had between them shared 15.9 per cent of the market. In 1980, before the J series front-wheel drive Cavalier was launched, the Cortina on its own commanded 12.6 per cent of the market. The repercussions for model volume are considerable. In the Cortina's Indian summer in 1979 and 1980, Ford sold more than 190,000 Cortinas each year on the UK market. But in the new market conditions, the medium class leader (the Cavalier) has never sold much more than 130,000 units on the UK market. Austin Rover's Montego, which was a late entrant into this class, will be lucky to claim UK sales of more than 75,000 a year.

Fragmentation is an extremely powerful force in the other classes although its chronology and extent are variable. In the small car class, market fragmentation set in early; the Ford Fiesta was established and had claimed 6 per cent of the market against the Mini before the Metro was launched in the autumn of 1980. Since then, market share has always been roughly equally divided between Ford's Fiesta and Austin's Metro, which in 1985 sold 6.8 per cent and 6.5 per cent of the market respectively. In this class, Vauxhall is the late entrant (as Austin was in the medium class) and the pattern again is that the last new model to be launched by a major takes a smaller but significant market share; the small Nova took 3.3 per cent of the market for Vauxhall in 1985. Again, this division of sales has inevitable repercussions for model volume. Even before the Nova was a force to be reckoned with, in 1983 Ford and Austin only sold 120,000 and 140,000 of their respective super-Minis on the British market. The presence of the Nova will further erode model volume in the small class. It is true that in the light class the position is rather different because Ford's Escort retains the 10 per cent magic and the old kind of class domination; with its booted variant, the Orion, the Escort captured no less than 12.1 per cent of the 1985 market. But this result can hardly be sustained. In the Orion Ford has produced a variant model which temporarily sustains flagging Escort sales; in the past two years the hatchback Escort has lost sales equivalent to 1.5 per cent of the market. Furthermore, for rather different reasons, both Austin and Vauxhall have weak offerings in this class. The Austin Maestro is a worthy but unexciting motor car and, more important, until 1985, the Vauxhall Astra was a first generation offering from GM; on past form, it will take two generations of product before Vauxhall wins 6 per cent or more for one model. It is unlikely that Ford can resist for long the pressures of market fragmentation in the light class.

The fragmentation of demand in the new era of direct competition not only has implications for model volume, it also has repercussions for market share. With a compact model range, any major company's overall market will be roughly equal to the sum of the market shares claimed by its three volume sellers. In the old days of indirect competition it was possible for a major to work the two-car trick, which involved taking 20 per cent of the British market with just two cars. BMC did this convincingly in the mid- and late 1960s with the Mini and the 1100/1300; while Ford more or less pulled the trick off throughout the period from the introduction of the Escort in 1967 to the run-out of the Cortina in 1982. As the 1985 top ten (Table 4.6) shows, Ford still manages the two-car trick with different models; the Escort/Orion and the Fiesta together took 18.9 per cent of the market in 1985. But that result depends on the sales success of the Escort/Orion and, as we have argued, the Escort/Orion is a unique model whose days of class dominance are probably numbered. In fact, as Table 4.7 shows, in the era of full-line direct competition it is becoming increasingly difficult to take 20 per cent of the market even with three models.

As harbinger of what is to come, it is instructive to look at the current achievement of Vauxhall and Austin Rover. With three volume models (the Cavalier, Astra and Nova), Vauxhall took just 14.8 per cent of the market in 1985. Astra and Nova take low shares because, as we have explained, they are late entrants or first-generation GM products in their market classes. But, if the second-

Table 4.7. Share of the British car market claimed by Austin Rover, Ford and Vauxhall's three best-selling models

	1975	1976	1977	1978	1979	1980	1981	1982	1983	1984	1985
Austin Rover	19.0	16.1	13.8	13.3	11.9	10.5	12.2	11.7	13.4	13.4	13.6
Ford	19.9	22.4	20.1	20.3	22.4	26.8	27.8	26.5	25.3	22.7	24.4
Vauxhall	7.3	8.3	8.4	7.8	6.0	6.0*	5.0*	10.9	12.0	13.9	14.8

Source: SMMT

*Two models only.

generation Astra and Nova are almost as successful as the Cavalier now is, then GM would still have to field three volume models to take 20 per cent of the market. The position of Austin Rover is even less favourable. In 1984 the company was represented in the small and light segments with two established models, Metro and Maestro, which together took 11.4 per cent of the market. The launch of Montego into the medium sector did not solve any substantial problem because that car poached sales and market share from the Maestro; in 1985, their first full sales year together, the three new models (Metro, Maestro and Montego) together took just 13.6 per cent of the market.

The market result which we observe at Austin Rover is more or less statistically inevitable under current market conditions of full-line direct competition. The basic position is that the three majors produce the top ten models and the top ten sell 50 per cent of the market; to be exact, the top ten models claimed 53 per cent of the market in 1985. There is a reasonably balanced distribution of sales between the different volume models of the majors; if the Escort/Orion is excluded, no single model from the majors sells more than 7.3 per cent or less than 3.1 per cent of the market. It is also true that the three market segments (small, light and medium) are now roughly equal in size. Under these conditions, an average volume model from a major will take about 5 per cent of the market and a range of three such volume models would take just 15 per cent of the market. Austin Rover's recovery strategy was doomed to fail on the British car market because three times five equals 15, well short of its target 24 or 25 per cent. Worse still, there was no guarantee that Austin Rover would achieve the average 15 per cent. In each market class, one or two class-leading models can sell around 7 per cent, but that ensures that the third best seller in the segment will only take about 3.5 per cent of the market. The nature of the fierce direct competition is such that no one major is likely to lead in all three market segments and it is difficult to avoid being pushed into third place in at least one market class. Austin Rover's misfortune is that it is currently in third place in two market segments; the Maestro is a poor third in the light class just as the Montego is in the medium class. From this kind of position, in the era of full-line direct competition, Austin Rover finds it impossible to obtain an average market share of 15 per cent with its three volume models.

If Austin Rover's home market share is constrained by the new pattern of full-line direct competition, the implications for total sales and individual model volume are fairly devastating. In recent years around 1,750,000 new cars have been sold annually in the UK, and a 15 per cent share of that national market translates into maximum sales of around 260,000 cars which can only be claimed by a major company which produces a full range of three models. Austin Rover could do little about these external limits on home market sales. If the company could not beat Ford, and it could not, then it would not be able to resist the force of market fragmentation. What Austin Rover could and should have done, was to develop export markets as a way of escaping the sales constraints of the home market. That is to say, the company should have responded like other European manufacturers who all face increasingly severe direct competition and fragmentation of their home markets; they respond by pushing product into near-European export markets so as to make good any losses sustained at home. The situation was one in which Austin Rover could have done something about exports. Although there were external market limitations on export sales, these limits could have been shifted by appropriate investment in distribution and marketing. Austin Rover's fate was sealed when nothing constructive was done in this crucial area and the company lost export sales when it desperately needed to increase them.

We have already noted the collapse in export sales at the end of the 1970s. Table 4.8 sets the recent performance of Austin Rover in a longer-term perspective. Austin Rover emerges badly from any comparison of its recent export performance with that of the volume car Austin Morris operation a decade earlier in the early 1970s. The most immediately notable feature is a substantial decline in the proportion of volume car output which was exported; from 1970 to 1973 inclusive, Austin Morris exported on average 43 per cent of output, while from 1980 to 1983 inclusive, Austin Rover exported on average just 28 per cent of what it produced. Any comparison also shows that lost export sales are the major cause of the overall decline in volume car output since the early 1970s. Austin car production fell from an average of 656,000 in the years 1970–3 to just 367,000 in the years 1980–3. The company's output of volume cars declined by 289,000 between the two periods and 178,000 lost export sales accounted for 62 per cent of the total output loss between these dates. The final point must be that any comparison between Austin Rover now and Austin Morris in the early 1970s understates the extent of the deterioration in the company's export performance. This arises because Austin Rover has closed the peripheral factories (Canley, Speke and Solihull) which produced specialist Rover and Triumph cars in significant quantities for home and export markets.

In the years 1970–3 the peripheral Rover and Triumph factories were largely responsible for a specialist output which averaged 206,000 cars per year in the period 1970–3. Because these factories, like volume cars in this period, exported around 40 per cent of what they made, specialist car exports amounted to an average of 81,000 cars a year in the period 1970–3. On the longer view, the post-1977 achievement was to reduce the exports of volume cars to the level at which specialist car exports had been running in the years before the change in management.

The remaining point which should be emphasised is that the collapse in export sales occurred during the short period when Michael Edwardes was chairman. Export volume and proportion of volume car output exported held up well in the late 1970s; on both counts, the company's performance in 1978 was fractionally better than its admittedly not very good performance in 1975. But, as the figures in Table 4.8 show, exports then fell in four of the five years when Michael Edwardes was chairman. The cumulative result was quite dramatic. In just five years the proportion of output exported was more or less halved from nearly 40 to just 20 per cent and export volumes were halved from 180,000 to 90,000. The availability of new models in recent years has not made any perceptible difference to export volumes; in 1984 the company allocated just 80,000 cars for export (*Financial Times*, 7 May 1985). As a consequence, a company whose home market sales were constrained by fragmentation lost export volume and became increasingly dependent on its home market.

It must be conceded that the company faced highly unfavourable conditions in all its export markets in the early 1980s. In particular, the Thatcher government's initial deep commitment in 1979 to tight monetary policies, reinforced by Britain's emergence as a major oil exporter, drove sterling up to very high levels on the foreign exchanges. As a result the relative price of British exports was increased (and imports into Britain became cheaper), which made conditions very difficult for British manufactures, as a chorus of distinguished industrialists later explained to the House of Lords Select Committee on Overseas Trade. In his autobiographical account, Sir Michael Edwardes naturally repeatedly stresses the problems which were created for BL by this additional barrier to restoring competitiveness: 'It was infuriating. Just as we got the business into a semblance of shape and order there would be another surge in the pound which yet again threw us off course' (Edwardes, 1983, p. 128). The reality of all this is not in question. Manufactur-

Table 4.8. BL car exports, 1970–85

(a) Austin Morris (volume car) production and exports, 1970–5

	Production (000s)	Exports (000s)	Output exported (%)
1970	588	279	47.4
1971	666	301	45.2
1972	698	275	39.4
1973	673	270	40.1
1974	561	249	44.4
1975	450	172	38.2

(b) Jaguar Rover Triumph (specialist car) production and exports, 1970–5

	Production (000s)	Exports (000s)	Output exported (%)
1970	201	89	44.3
1971	203	85	41.9
1972	219	73	33.3
1973	203	78	38.4
1974	178	74	41.6
1975	155	84	54.2

(c) Austin Rover production and exports 1978–83

	Production (000s)	Exports (000s)	Output exported (%)
1978	466	183	39.3
1979	388	144	37.1
1980	315	119	37.8
1981	348	95	27.3
1982	370	108	29.2
1983	433	88	20.3

Source: SMMT, *Annual Statistics*.

ing industry suffered severely and the problems were particularly acute for a precariously poised company like BL. What can be questioned, however, is the nature of the company's strategic response. It was this which determined not just the extent to which the company lost export sales under the high sterling rates of 1980–1, but the failure to retake this lost ground as the pound later fell in value.

If we are going to analyse the export strategy, we must begin by recognising that poor export performance at Austin Rover is the result of variable performance in different national markets which presented different opportunities and problems. It is appropriat therefore, to discuss the company's export performance in its m markets. In the late 1970s, the company had two major markets: North America, where it sold nearly 70,000 sports cars each year, and Europe, where it sold twice as many saloons.

The North American market was a problem mainly because here the company had to sell a specialist product directly against the Japanese. The MGB was out of date and the company's new sports car of the late 1970s, the TR7, was resoundingly beaten in the American market-place by the Datsun 240/260Z. Austin Rover never really had the resources to stay in this game; the company could not afford to develop new sports cars and its manufacturing facilities were too inflexible to build sports cars and saloons on the same lines. The Edwardes team therefore decided to pull out of the US market; only Jaguar kept a toehold in this market. On the other hand, the European market was an opportunity because the Japanese were shut out from several of the major national markets such as Italy and France and because the European market would take the new saloon and hatchback models which the Edwardes team had developed. The company could and should have aimed to win extra volume by taking 3–5 per cent of the European market, as the Ryder Report envisaged it would. As we have noted, the company ended up with well under 1 per cent of the European market. The results in terms of volume of car exports to Europe are really dispiriting, as Table 4.9 shows. Far from increasing or maintaining European exports, the volume of exports to Europe was more or less halved between 1977 and 1983. The failure to exploit European export opportunities is the main cause of Austin's poor export performance during these years.

Table 4.9. BL car exports to the EEC, 1976–83 (thousands)

Year	Exports
1976	155
1977	168
1978	159
1979	120
1980	111
1981	92
1982	86
1983	77

MMT, *Annual Statistics*

70s Austin Morris's performance in European export depended on the export of kits rather than fully The old BMC had gone into Europe quite effectively by setting up assembly operations in Spain, Italy and Belgium (Williams *et al.*, 1983, p. 237). But the company had never owned or controlled the Spanish and Italian assembly operations; and by the time Michael Edwardes took over, the Spanish deal had lapsed and the Italian deal was turning sour as Innocenti rebodied the Mini and turned to buy their engines and gearboxes from Daihatsu of Japan. That left the company, by the beginning of the 1980s, very dependent on the one European assembly plant which it did own at Seneffe in Belgium, where Minis and Allegros were assembled. In 1981 the company decided to close this plant. The collapse of the Italian deal and the closure of Seneffe had a quite disastrous effect on Austin Rover's export volumes. In 1977 BL exported 76,000 built-up cars to Europe and 114,000 knocked-down kits; in 1982 the comparable figures were 90,000 and 3,000 (Jones, 1985a, p. 167). The huge fall in European exports was statistically accounted for by the disappearance of kit shipments. The same conclusion emerges from an examination of BL car sales figures in European markets which are given in Table 4.10. About half of BL sales to Europe in the late 1970s were taken in Belgium and most of the rest were taken in Italy. Sales in these two markets depended on local assembly which gave Austin's small cars the status of semi-indigenous products; without the benefit of this status, export sales in Belgium and Italy collapsed.

Table 4.10. BL car exports to the EEC, by country, 1976–83

	1976	1977	1978	1979	1980	1981	1982	1983
Belgium/Lux	80,121	82,233	83,919	53,647	38,265	5,478	14,752	7,990
Denmark	20,212	8,516	3,750	1,619	236	685	94	416
France	7,836	7,325	5,463	6,529	6,435	21,988	34,453	34,118
Germany	9,181	7,068	9,371	4,530	5,429	5,474	2,969	7,535
Greece	3,370	378	108	13	8	5	8	4
Ireland	6,630	7,129	6,093	2,209	2,276	2,931	2,696	2,979
Italy	17,165	47,063	43,477	46,962	54,789	50,002	28,495	16,583
Netherlands	10,208	8,927	7,209	4,776	3,772	5,302	2,269	7,194
Total EEC	154,723	168,639	159,390	120,285	111,210	91,865	85,736	76,819

Source: SMMT, *Annual Statistics*

The closure of Seneffe signified the emergence of a new export strategy; Austin Rover in the early 1980s aimed to shift from local assembly in European factories to direct export from British factories. The failure of this strategy accounts for the company's poor export performance in the first half of the 1980s. In many ways the strategy of direct export was immediately attractive. The kits embodied less British content and value added than did fully built-up cars. And the facility at Longbridge which built the Metro would always be underutilised if it depended on home market sales. But the strategy of switching to direct exports encountered two major problems. First, by 1981 the pound was rising ever higher and the profitability of direct exports of fully built-up cars was much more vulnerable to a high pound; on kits, the company only suffered the penalty of a high pound on the components which originated in Britain and the effects of that could have been palliated by suitable transfer-pricing arrangements. Second, before or after 1981, export volumes could not be maintained after the company's product lost semi-indigenous status in Belgium or Italy because in most European countries Austin Rover did not have a proper distribution network.

For these two reasons, after 1981 the company got the worst of all possible worlds in terms of export volumes and profits. As Edwardes justly complained in his autobiography, the high pound made direct exports from British factories unprofitable. And, in this situation, the company seems not to have struggled unduly to win export volume. Indeed, in the early 1980s, Austin Rover deliberately pulled out of many of the smaller markets like Denmark. And the company did not recoup its position by fighting aggressively in the three major national markets (West Germany, France and Italy) where more than 5 million new cars are sold each year. France was a partial exception which shows that the company could probably have made more export sales if it had committed more resources to the task; Austin Rover sales on the French market rose from nearly 8,000 in 1977 to just over 34,000 in 1983, the increase coinciding with the launch of the Metro. But in West Germany, the largest national car market in Europe, sales were small and — at best — stagnant. Here Austin Rover has fairly consistently held a market share of just 0.2 per cent. In 1982, the company claimed to have 280 dealers in Germany selling a range including the Metro and yet the German dealer network sold just 6,000 cars in that year (*Financial Times*, 28 February 1983). The implication must be that in this period Austin's German distribution network really existed only on paper; a weak European importer like Fiat with a dealer network of that size in Britain would expect to sell around 50,000 cars a year. With some justice, the *Financial Times* (16 October 1984) interpreted a decline in European sales in 1984 as evidence that 'Austin Rover's dealer network on the continent is too weak to take advantage' of new products like Metro and Maestro.

When the company faced insuperable limits on home sales, the neglect of export markets was a fatal miscalculation; whatever else the company did or did not do, these miscalculations guaranteed the failure of the recovery strategy. It is therefore worth analysing the nature of the miscalculation. If the company made poor decisions about markets and marketing, why did it do so? More exactly, by what process of faulty reasoning did management make its miscalculation?

Clearly, all the miscalculations stemmed from management's failure to recognise the limits on home market sales established by increasing market fragmentation in a new era of full-line direct competition; if the management team had appreciated the extent of these limits at home, then exports would have been tackled as a matter of urgent priority because the company was increasingly in an export-or-die crisis. However, it could reasonably be argued in defence that the full extent of this was not so obvious in the late 1970s when it was difficult to foresee the degree to which direct competition would fragment the market in the light and medium classes of the car market; even Vauxhall was surprised by the success of the J series Cavalier in the medium class after 1981. But, as we have noted, in the small car class the market fragmentation had already taken place with the introduction of the Fiesta before the Metro was launched in autumn 1980. The implications for Metro sales could and should have been taken on board but they were not because the company had privileged the product in a somewhat uncritical fashion rather than analysed the market in a more sober way; management was misled by its romantic faith in the market-conquering sales potential of the new product. This is reflected in the curious way Michael Edwardes glossed over the issue in his autobiography. With no supporting evidence or figures Metro is simply presented as an export success: it 'quickly established itself as our top-seller in Europe' (Edwardes, 1983, p. 185).

It is symptomatic of priorities in the later 1970s that the new team restyled the product but did not revise the sales estimates before Metro was launched. When Michael Edwardes took over in 1977, the company had the results of consumer 'clinics' which compared prototypes of the Mini replacement with the then newly launched Ford Fiesta and VW Polo. The new chairman was so disturbed by adverse consumer reaction to the Austin prototype that he ordered a complete restyling of the car which delayed the Metro's launch by a full twelve months. But Michael Edwardes and his team never took on board the basic point that the existence of the Fiesta and Polo in the market-place would inevitably fragment sales in the small car class. Crucially, they never revised Metro sales estimates of 350,000 plus which dated from the early 1970s (Willman and Winch, 1985, p. viii) when BL dominated the small car class at home and was only challenged by Renault and Fiat's super-Minis in Europe. These sales estimates were quite unrealistic in 1978 when Ford and VW had already entered the small car class and Vauxhall/Opel's entrance was only being delayed by GM's decision to build its small car in an all-new Spanish factory. Thanks mainly to opposition from the Fiesta on the British market, Austin Rover has never sold more than 170,000 Metros a year, or half as many as planned.

Export sales were essential if the Metro or later models were to sell in decent volume. But under the new management, the company in effect, though not in rhetoric, treated the European export business as an optional extra. The recurrent complaint was that a high pound in the early 1980s made the export business difficult. As Edwardes said to a Commons select committee in 1981,

> marketing effort, quality specification and reliability all play a part and some of our products are not good enough to sell in certain markets. I accept that but you can take it from me the bulk of the problems against Land Rovers and cars can be met by getting to the right exchange rate without which we either make no profit or cut whole markets (House of Commons Trade and Industry Select Committee, 1981, minutes of evidence, Q. 138).

Faced with this dilemma, the management effectively decided to 'cut markets' including European car markets; as we have seen, in the early 1980s, they pulled out of some smaller national markets and made an inadequate effort in the larger ones. The retreat from export business which was, at least in the short run, unprofitable reflected a fundamental misunderstanding of the general role of exports in the European car business and the particular importance of exports for Austin Rover. Since the late 1950s (Maxcy and Silbertson, 1959) intra-European exports have been a marginally profitable (or unprofitable) business for many European volume car producers. But these companies take on and pursue the business because although unit profit per car sold is not attractive, export business helps by loading the factories and raising model volume. This form of calculation applied with particular force to a company with Austin Rover's problems in the early 1980s. In so far as the company withdrew to the home market where sales were constrained, Austin Rover inevitably suffered from underutilised factories and low model volume; given the company's weakness at home, the policy of market retreat abroad put the company in a position where it could never make a profit. In the early 1980s, therefore, the company disastrously failed to exploit the only market opportunity which could have secured its future as an independent car manufacturer.

Even if the company had decided on a policy of short-term market retreat, Austin Rover should have defended and developed its distribution network in the larger European national markets because the existence of that network was the precondition for selling cars in Europe in the medium and longer term. Mainland European sales could only be increased in the future if Austin Rover systematically undertook expense investment on dealer development and support, parts back-up, advertising to establish the new products, and aggressive new entrant pricing. Amazingly, this kind of expense investment was never budgeted for. Although the enterprise obtained more than £2,000 million of public funds, the company does not seem to have asked for, or obtained, any funds which were specifically earmarked for marketing. Expense investment on European marketing certainly never figured as an objective in the recovery plan which concentrated on three areas — investment in new product, investment in process technology and reform of industrial relations. Expense investment on European marketing is the crucial missing fourth objective. After all, the company might have new product produced by a docile labour force in automated factories, but the hard fact was that it would never get a decent return on all this effort, if it neglected expense investment in European marketing which was the essential precondition if it was to sell, and thus produce, the new models in decent volume.

The need for such expense investment was never recognised because the company assumed that under the right conditions new product would sell itself in Europe. This point emerges indirectly from Sir Michael Edwardes's autobiography. In this he reasonably complains about the damaging effect on exports in the early 1980s of a high pound and restrictions on Austin exports to countries like Spain, which was not then in the EEC free trade area (Edwardes, 1983, p. 269). Edwardes was never explicit, but the logic of his position was that, in so far as the exchange rate was right and trade barriers were removed, then exports to Europe would not be a problem. This hypothesis has been disproved by disappointing car export sales to France, West Germany, Italy and other EEC markets in the past couple of years with a low pound. The strategy of the early 1980s, which involved a switch to direct exports without the commitment of resources to selling the product in Europe, reflected a fundamental misunderstanding about the nature of the cars business; differentiated consumer products like cars will only sell if supported by a proper marketing effort and that requires generous expense investment funding. It was true that home sales needed relatively little marketing effort. But that was because in the UK the company had a proper distribution network which could at least sell into the private sector. With this network in place, the marketing men's job was mainly to place the adverts for successive 'campaigns' in which Austin Rover discounted the product in an attempt to shift it from the showrooms. Without a proper distribution network in Europe, a constructive marketing effort was needed and the company did not budget for that because it seems not to have appreciated the importance of expense investment in marketing.

It is not clear that the company's later management learned the lesson about the need for export marketing in Europe. In the first part of 1986, Austin Rover made a disproportionate fuss about large percentage increases from low sales bases in some of the smaller national markets such as Portugal, and the company was quietly re-entering some of the smaller markets such as Denmark which had earlier been abandoned. But Austin Rover had still put very little effort or money into sorting out distribution in the major European national markets where the company's position was as weak as ever.

The problems of German distribution have not been constructively resolved since 1982 even though the company now identifies Germany as 'a key target for the company and the prime target for its development plans' (*Autocar*, 18 September 1985). In the autumn of 1984, it was reported that Austin Rover had signed a deal with the German Massa hypermarket chain which would sell Austin Rover cars as 'own brand products' from twenty-two of its sites (*Financial Times*, 16 October 1984). This kind of attempt to bypass orthodox distribution channels seldom works in the cars business because of problems about trade-in facilities as well as parts and service back-up. It is a desperate measure which appeals to a marginal firm which is so weak that it cannot build a dealer network. There is an analogy in the current British motorbike market where the Japanese firms have the market sewn up and the Yugoslav moped producer, Tomas, tries to sell through Woolworth and mail-order catalogues.

This is the kind of position which Austin Rover seeks to occupy in the West German car market. Not surprisingly, the results so far have been disappointing. It was initially reported that Austin Rover's 'stated target' was 1 per cent of the German market or 25,000 cars by 1985 (*Autocar*, 7 November 1984). But almost immediately the script was changed and the sales target was revised downwards; after Massa started selling the cars, the target became 8,000 cars, which the company did sell in West Germany in 1985 (*Autocar*, 21 November 1984; *Financial Times*, 11 September 1985). In an Austin Rover press release this would no doubt be described as a 33 per cent improvement on 1982 sales; by any other standard this kind of volume represents total failure.

By mid-1986, the company's export marketing efforts were concentrated on the United States, where the company planned to sell the new Rover 800 large saloon under the Sterling badge. It is encouraging to learn that the current BL five-year plan includes provision for the expense of marketing this car through a new American dealer network which will be 100 strong (*Autocar*, 14 August 1985). But, despite a good start, it must be doubtful whether the company will derive the full benefit from this initiative because it will not now be easy to break into the lucrative but highly competitive American luxury saloon market. The West Germans have a very strong established position in this market; the four German marques of Mercedes, BMW, Audi and Porsche sell more than 250,000 luxury saloons each year in the United States and between them take one-third of the market for saloons costing over $16,000 (*Financial Times*, 18 March 1986). At the same time, the Japanese firms are moving up-market to challenge the Germans. The new Rover has been jointly developed with Honda which will start selling its version of the car some eight months ahead of Sterling in the American market. Customers who wait for the British model will pay about $2,000 more for a car whose main selling feature will be a traditional British leather and wood interior. If all goes well, Austin Rover expects to sell around 20,000 cars per year in the American market (*Financial Times*, 9 May 1985; *Autocar*, 14 August 1985). Even if all goes well, and even on the updated target of 30,000 in mid-1986, such sales will not release the company from the constraint of low model volume. Past experience of big Rover sales in the UK suggests that the company will be lucky to sell more than 25,000 of the new Rover each year on the home market. It seems likely that the company will sell relatively few big Rovers in Europe because it has not sorted out distribution in West Germany, which is the only sizeable national market for large saloons in Europe. Rover model volume of around 50,000 each year is simply not enough when specialists like Mercedes or Volvo and mass producers like Ford are making their big executive saloons at a rate of 150,000 per annum or more. The deficit in volume is such that Austin Rover must depend heavily on the deal whereby it shares the new Rover's development costs with Honda and will in due course assemble Honda's version of the car for sale by Honda in Europe.

The concentration on the American export market is an index of a subtle shift in the company's marketing strategy. The company has now lost the opportunity to use large export sales as a defence for an Austin Rover manufacturing operation producing the current generation of models; that opportunity is lost because if the company were in 1986 to decide to build up the European dealer network, the existing models would be near replacement and running out on the production lines by the time such a dealer network was selling product in significant quantity. The Rover 800 case suggests that the company will now try to take small export sales as an adjunct to its strategy of simply assembling the next generation of Hondas. The irony is, of course, that this assembly strategy is itself necessitated by the market pressures which have undermined the company's plans for the recovery of car manufacture. As Table 4.11 shows, the pressure of market fragmentation at home and the failure to exploit European market opportunities together ensure that the company does not have respectable production volume on any of its current models. In 1984 Metro production sagged below 150,000 and the Maestro and Montego were being jointly produced at similar volume.

Table 4.11. Production volumes at Austin Rover, 1982–4 (thousands)

	1982	1983	1984
Metro	174	175	145
Maestro	2	102	81
Montego	—	—	59
Acclaim	58	50	32
Mini	52	49	35
Rover SD1	33	34	—

This conclusion illustrates the point that the market pressures which have undermined the strategy for the recovery of car manufacture are now pushing the firm towards assembly. The shape of things to come is indicated by the Triumph Acclaim/Rover 213; this car is a Honda Ballade, a booted version of the Civic, which was originally assembled by Austin Rover at a rate of 50,000 per annum with production volume sagging to little more than 30,000 units in 1984. Assembly can be profitable at this kind of volume, but manufacture is out of the question. Rover's existing volume offerings in the small, light and medium classes (the Metro, Maestro and Montego) will all be replaced, after 1989, with new models which are being 'jointly developed' with Honda. Agreement has already been reached to develop a new middle-range car, code-named YY, to replace the Maestro and Rover 213 models (*Financial Times*, 5 June 1985). This joint-development formula puts a brave face on the company's demotion to the status of a client assembler of another manufacturer's cars. The remaining political uncertainty is simply whether Austin Rover management is allowed to continue with its long-preferred strategy of assembling Hondas; if the company were sold to another manufacturer, like Ford, the Honda deal would lapse and the new purchaser would supply different kits for assembly. But one way or another, demotion to assembly seems inevitable without some form of intervention because the maintenance of a manufacturing operation depends on the attainment of volume sales which the company cannot find on the British home market, where it is pinned down, and because it does not have a European distribution network.

The final question is to what extent can an assembly strategy succeed under present market conditions? This issue is important because, as we shall argue in the next chapter, in terms of value added and employment in the car factory and at the component suppliers one assembled kit car from Japan is less valuable than one British manufactured car; around one half the value added in a kit car will be British whereas the Maestro and Montego are 80 per cent British and the Metro is more than 90 per cent British. But, if Austin Rover succeeds in selling substantially more kit cars than it did of its own manufactured cars, there could well be a net benefit in terms of value added and employment at Longbridge and Cowley as well as in the component factories. In this context it is important that Honda is offering to do more than supply direct replacements for the Metro, Maestro and Montego; in the summer of 1985 it was reported that Honda would supply 'extra' models and that up to 100,000 of these extra models could be assembled at Austin Rover factories (*Financial Times*, 5 June 1985). The government was then pressing Austin Rover to take up this option. It is not possible to be certain about how extra assembled Honda models will sell, partly because it is not clear whether and to what extent Honda's European dealer network can or will sell Austin Rover assembled cars. But it is clear that, under present market conditions, extra models will not smoothly raise Austin Rover's home market share to 25 per cent or more. This is because, over the past twenty years, as competition has intensified Austin Rover has been increasingly pushed down and out of the top ten positions in the UK sales charts.

Austin Rover has long been marginalised in terms of top three sales. The last Austin Morris product which could regularly take number one position in the sales charts was the Austin 1100/1300 until its sales were spoiled by the short-lived sales success of its stable companion, the Marina, in the early 1970s. For the decade from 1972 to 1982 inclusive, Ford's Escort and Cortina took number one and two positions with monotonous regularity. As Table 4.12 shows, Austin Morris did claim the number three position with the Marina or Mini in the later 1970s; and the Metro did this same job for the company in the three years after it was launched in the early 1980s. But this third place position is hardly secure because the Mini did not make the top three in its last full year of volume sales in 1980 and, in a highly competitive market, the middle-aged Metro did not make the top three in 1984 or 1985. In three of the six sales years from 1980 Austin Rover has had no car in the top three.

Migration down the top three was not immediately disastrous because the company in the mid-1970s fielded a variety of models which won useful sales for the company by capturing many of the lower positions in the top ten; as Table 4.12 shows, in the four years 1973 to 1976, the company captured four or five of the bottom seven places as well as regularly claiming number three position. In this period, the low-volume models like the Dolomite, Maxi and Princess helped the company considerably in terms of volume and market share; for example, in 1974, when the Dolomite, Maxi and Princess occupied positions seven, nine and ten, this won the company 106,000 sales which was equal to 8.3 per cent of the market in that year. Austin could not maintain its market position in this way because from 1977 onwards it never managed to get more than three cars into the top ten in any one year. For this reason, 1977 was a turning point in the company's decline. Immediately after the company was reduced to three models in the top ten, its market share fell to levels from which it has never recovered; the BL cars market share fell below 25 per cent for the first time and the Austin Morris share sank to its normal post-1977 level of 18.5 per cent. As we have explained, under current market conditions of direct com-

Table 4.12. BL models in the top ten sales positions, 1972–85

	1972	1973	1974	1975	1976	1977	1978
1							
2		Marina					
3	Marina		Mini	Mini	Mini	Marina	Marina
4	1100/1300		Marina	Marina	Marina	Mini	Mini
5		Mini	Allegro	Allegro	Allegro	Allegro	
6	Mini						Allegro
7			Dolomite				
8	Maxi	1100/1300		Dolomite	Maxi		
9		Dolomite	Maxi	Princess	Princess		
10		Maxi	Princess				
	1979	**1980**	**1981**	**1982**	**1983**	**1984**	**1985**
1							
2							
3	Mini		Metro	Metro	Metro		
4	Marina	Mini	Ital			Metro	Metro
5	Allegro	Marina					
6					Maestro	Maestro	
7				Acclaim			Montego
8		Allegro			Acclaim		
9							
10			Mini				Maestro

Source: SMMT, *Annual Statistics*

petition, the company's market share cannot recover as long as it has so few cars in the top ten. Austin Rover has not been able to score more than three places in the top ten for two reasons. First, under the management's compact model range plan, the old low-volume models like Dolomite and Maxi were discontinued and the company did not have enough light and medium models to claim six places. Second, in an era of full-line direct competition, the positions in the top ten which would once have been occupied by the multiplicity of low-volume BL models are now occupied by offerings from the other majors; from 1977 to 1984 Ford and Vauxhall together claimed six out of the top ten sales places and in 1985 they claimed seven out of the first ten places. In this situation, even if Austin Rover broadens its range by assembling more Honda models, it is unlikely that the company will ever be able to claim more than four places in the top ten.

Austin Rover's position is rather worse than this conclusion suggests because the company is still poaching its own sales when it introduces new models. When the company pushes a new model into the top ten, it tends to displace one of its existing models which is already in the top ten. The introduction of Maestro and Montego evicted the Triumph Acclaim/Rover 213 from the top ten in which it had figured in both 1982 and 1983. This displacement effect is quite strong because, rather disturbingly from the company's point of view, Austin Rover's three volume models are increasingly stuck in the lower reaches of the top ten. In five of the six years from 1974 to 1979, the company managed to get some combination of its three volume sellers (the Mini, Marina and Allegro) into positions three, four and five in the sales charts. In 1985, when the company had the full range of models on sale for the whole year, the Metro claimed position four, the newly launched Montego did no better than position seven and the Maestro just scraped in at position ten. It is remarkable that, in its second full year on the market, Austin Rover's light car (the Maestro) could only capture 3.2 per cent of the market with total home sales of less than 60,000. The probability is that if Austin Rover assembles new models from Honda or any other manufacturer, these models will sell at the 25,000–35,000 level, the level now achieved by imported cars like the Volvo 340 or VW Polo as well as the Rover 213. If the new assembled models do any better than this, they are likely to do so by reducing Maestro and Montego to this kind of sales volume.

Before Michael Edwardes became chairman, the company claimed its market share by manufacturing too many old models; in the late 1960s, BL had to make nineteen different body shells to claim 40 per cent of the home market when Ford took 25 per cent of the home market with just three body shells. After the late 1970s recovery plan, under new market conditions of fragmentation and direct competition, Austin Rover had too few new models to claim a market share of 25 per cent. But the addition of extra assembled Honda models does not offer an easy way of achieving this target because the same market pressures which drive the company towards assembly ensure that the volume benefits from a broader Austin range willl be small. In this case, assembly is unlikely to benefit value added and employment and, even at this late stage, it is worth thinking about how to defend and preserve a genuine car manufacturing capability. This is the issue which we examine in our next chapter.

5/No End of a Lesson

The argument and analysis so far has been very specific; the previous chapters have been more or less exclusively preoccupied with the actions of management in one division of a giant enterprise. This was necessary when our primary aim was to produce a case study of a business strategy and its failure. At the same time, although case-study material is inherently interesting, the results of any particular study will only be significant if the material has a broader pertinence and relevance. Our study of Austin Rover meets this significance requirement. There is much in the autobiographical account given by Sir Michael Edwardes with which we would disagree, but on one point we are in complete agreement; BL, he wrote, 'deserves a record which explores the complexity of the problems and pressures, for BL presents a microcosm of the issues affecting British industry as a whole' (Edwardes, 1983, p. 9). The predicament of the BL Cars division was, and is, similar to that of many other major British companies in the manufacturing sector. More than this, the failure of Austin Rover's strategy focuses attention on the role of government policy and, more specifically, on the limits of Thatcherite microeconomics as a way of dealing with British industrial decline. In the first half of this concluding chapter we will extend the scope of the discussion to establish connections with broader issues.

When these connections have been established, we will turn in the second half of this chapter to the issue of what is to be done. New policy proposals are necessary because, without them, a case study of enterprise failure in a declining manufacturing sector must lead towards defeatism. Many readers will have difficulty in accepting our proposals, which require a partial break with European free trade. This may be heretical but we cannot repent or recant the minor heresy of safeguarding when the worsening British crisis requires radical new policy initiatives (see Cutler *et al.*, 1986) to deal with the trade problem. It is especially important to raise these policy issues in this chapter because we would not wish to leave our readers with the impression that this book is simply an attack on the competence of management and that the lesson of the failure at

Austin Rover is that the only thing we need is better managers. That would always help but in itself is not enough because government must also create an appropriate national environment in which purposive management can operate efficiently; only after political initiatives have safeguarded the home market can management and labour tackle productive problems which they can solve and market opportunities which they can exploit. To give Mrs Thatcher's government its due, it recognised the need to create an appropriate environment in which management could operate. But Thatcherism never identified the necessary environmental changes because it misrepresented the problems of manufacturing and exaggerated what management could do.

In the ideology of Thatcherism, industrial decline is attributed to a labour and wage problem which manifests itself in low productivity and poor cost competitiveness. As it happens this general view was put into the specific BL context by the Prime Minister's personal economic adviser, Professor (now Sir) Alan Walters, shortly after his appointment early in 1981. At a meeting with senior BL executives he expounded the view

> That the closure of BL, whether as the result of a strike or in cold blood, could have a positive effect on the British economy within six months. The short-term impact on regions such as the West Midlands and on the balance of payments might soon be offset . . . by the beneficial effect of the shock of closure on trades union and employee attitudes across the country. Restrictive practices would be swept away, pay increases would be held down and a more rapid improvement in Britain's competitiveness would thus be achieved through the closure of BL than by any other means available to the Government (Edwardes, 1983, pp. 205–6).

Walters proposed the destructive policy of the short sharp shock but the government, although it generally honoured right-wing market economists, did not on this occasion take their policy advice. In 1981, the government restated its support for the constructive policy of supporting management's efforts to turn the cars division round. In these microeconomic terms, Austin Rover's management was already doing the right things inside the cars division; strategies of labour reform, process innovation and product-led recovery were the only viable option for British manufacturing. The government should not, and could not, solve such microeconomic problems; and the government's macroeconomic responsibilities were the limited ones of lowering inflation and stimulating competition. From this point of view, the renaissance of British manufacturing depended on a change in management culture and in particular on a reassertion of the 'right to manage'.

The government was therefore able to take a very relaxed view of what many would regard as disturbing trends in Britain's overall economic performance. A joint permanent secretary at the Department of Trade and Industry, Sir Anthony Rawlinson, was pressed by a parliamentary committee about the rapid emergence of a huge deficit on trade in manufactures in the 1980s. He was able to respond:

> I think it is true that at any rate at official level we do not regard the emergence of a deficit on manufactures as in itself terribly worrying. We are concerned by the evidence which it provides of a failure of competitiveness . . . One of the themes of current ministerial policy . . . is that there is a limit to the role of Government in this area. The main contribution comes from macro-policies, notably getting down inflation and stimulating competition. (House of Lords Select Committee on Overseas Trade, 20 November 1984, Q.50).

When questioned by the same committee, the Chancellor strongly indicated the importance the government attached to shifting responsibility back to the enterprises:

> There was a time when those responsible for economic policy were concerned solely with the demand side of the equation. It was just a question of how much money you pumped into the economy, how big a deficit you had on the budget . . . I think we have all of us . . . moved away from that, and quite rightly, towards looking at what economists call the supply side, the nitty-gritty, how we can get the economy to perform better, how companies can become more efficient, how we can get better trade union behaviour, which is an important element in all this. I think these are the fundamental problems which we should be concerned about . . . there are ways in which the British economy has not been sufficiently dynamic or sufficiently competitive, where the trade unions and the labour market generally have been highly inflexible, and management in many cases has not been up to the mark (House of Lords, Select Committee on Overseas Trade, 15 May 1985, Q. 1697).

It would be wrong to represent the BL management as uncritical admirers of these policies. In the Bank of England's view, the attack on inflation through a tight control of the money supply was largely responsible for the sharp rise in the external value of the pound in the early 1980s (House of Lords, Select Committee on Overseas Trade, 1984–5, Q. 213, 215; *Bank of England Quarterly*, December

1981). Although the Edwardes autobiography does not much discuss the political causes of a high pound, it does repeatedly complain about its economic effects; as we have seen, the company's explanation of the poor export performance was the high pound which made exporting difficult. Nevertheless, at BL after 1977, considerable emphasis was placed on a change in management culture and the whole strategy rested on the assumption that, once management had reasserted the right to manage, management would be able to solve the problems of the enterprise at the level of the enterprise. In this respect, the company's strategy was impeccably Thatcherite even before her electoral triumph in 1979.

The reassertion of managerial authority is a unifying theme which runs through Sir Michael Edwardes's account of his years at BL. In the years leading up to his appointment in 1977 his belief was that 'management simply lost control of the situation . . . lost their will to manage' (Edwardes, 1983, p. 281). And thus 'very soon we realised that the *sine qua non* of survival was to re-establish the right to manage' (Edwardes, 1983, p. 52), 'restore authority to the factories, rebuilding the roles of factory managers, superintendents and foremen' (Edwardes, 1983, p. 55). The essential arena for the exercise of managerial authority is equally clearly stated: 'to regain the management role would mean counteracting shop steward power, which had got out of hand' (Edwardes, 1983, p. 74), so that 'everything which we did in employee relations was tested against the broad strategy of regaining management control of the business' (Edwardes, 1983, p. 161). A shift in managerial culture was needed to change 'the attitudes of managers who had grown up in an atmosphere of compromise and conciliation' (Edwardes, 1983, p. 75), and this could only be done from above because 'everything flows from the top' (Edwardes, 1983, p. 79). It would be no exaggeration to say that in his autobiography Sir Michael Edwardes presents management as the triumph of will.

The fate of the post-1977 strategy represents a test of such microeconomics. Indeed in many ways it is a crucial test because, as we will now argue, the strategy failed for reasons and under circumstances which are typical across large areas of British manufacturing. Failure was inevitable because the strategy at Austin Rover did not identify and engage with those conditions. Or, to put it another way, the point is that the assertion of the will to manage is not an end in itself nor sufficient to do the trick on its own. Management can only promote industrial recovery on two further conditions: first, management must formulate a strategy which identifies and attacks the real problems of the business in a sensible order, and second, the enterprise must be operating in an environment where the relevant internal and external problems can be solved by management. Neither of these conditions was satisfied at Austin Rover or in British manufacturing as a whole.

The preoccupation with labour at Austin Rover did not represent a diversion on to an imaginary problem. Chapter 2 showed that the company in 1977 had major problems about overmanning and work practices which in the short run cost it a lot of money and in the long run might have prevented (or at least hindered) the company from exploiting new technology. But the company's strategists should have realised that the benefits obtained from solving this one problem depended on the company's ability to solve other productive and market problems at the same time. Sir Michael Edwardes gives accounts of at least three major strategy reviews conducted by the company during his chairmanship — the Post House Hotel meeting at Christmas 1977, the recovery programme for 1980 and the Marlow Concept of mid-1980 (Edwardes, 1983, pp. 62–3, 97–9, 128–31). None of these reviews seems to have clearly established the labour problem as one in a hierarchy of interrelated problems which should be tackled in some definite order of priority. To judge from the company's actions and from the detailed account given later by Sir Michael Edwardes, solving the labour problem had an unjustifiable absolute priority and other pressing problems, for example in marketing, were not tackled with the same urgency and determination. For this reason, outstanding success in the reform of work practices failed to translate into overall productivity and profit. Reform of work practices created the potential for company-wide productivity increases but these could not be realised when the company did not confront and solve market problems which prevented the company from achieving continuous high-volume production.

The misordering of strategic priorities seems to have been a general failing of management in the first half of the 1980s; and in a great many cases the problem which has been unreasonably privileged is that of labour. There was a labour problem but, as has been argued elsewhere, labour problems were not in most cases the most serious source of competitive disadvantage (see Williams *et al.*, 1983, pp. 34–47). Labour costs often represented only a minor part of total costs and British labour was relatively cheap in European terms, so that lower performance was already reflected in lower rewards. In some sectors small scale imposed a greater cost handicap. In many more the real problems concerned the non-price characteristics of industrial output. These factors — design, quality, delivery, and so on, — are matters of managerial prerogative and they largely depend on management's ability to organise the scale and flow of production and on management's commitment to marketing. The combined effects of mass unemployment and trade-union legislation should not be overestimated (Batstone, 1984). But there can be no doubt that these developments have to some extent weakened the capacity of unionised labour to resist management. In capitalist production, labour prerogatives and practices are a secondary obstruction and in the British national economy they have become a minor secondary obstruction. The quality of the result in manufacturing depends on management's capacity to organise production and marketing; if management does not have a realistic broader strategy, then a competent and docile work-force is worth relatively little.

The failure of the business strategy at Austin Rover can clearly be attributed to faulty management decisions on the organisation of production and, above all, marketing. Here again the particular exemplifies and illustrates a more general problem. Austin Rover made life more difficult for itself by choosing dedicated automation at Longbridge; when the Metro did not sell at the planned rate, the company was left with underutilised and unusable excess capacity. That particular mistake may not have been repeated elsewhere in British industry but there is more general evidence of a mistaken belief that productive efficiency can be bought by investing in new machinery. In nationalised coal and steel, as well as cars, when managers were offered large quantities of state funding, they invested in inflexible high fixed-cost giantism like British Coal's super-pits or BSC's basic oxygen steel conventers (Williams, *et al.*, 1986). British managers in the private sector do not do much better with their more limited resources. In the last decade surveys have shown that the equipment in British factories is as modern and sophisticated as that in the factories of our European competitors; but there is much evidence that the equipment in British factories is often not well chosen for the particular task, is not well used or maintained and is frequently badly laid out (Daley, *et al.*, 1985). The disorganisation of production across large areas of British industry is such that investment in high technology is likely to be of limited benefit unless and until management is given better training in appraising and applying new productive methods.

In Austin Rover the crucial mistake was not so much the choice of inappropriate production technology as the failure to realise that this investment would only pay off if markets were secured. The central strategic blunder was the failure to give a high priority to marketing in a situation where market limitations were an increasingly threatening problem. Since the late nineteenth century, critics have alleged that British manufacturers neglect marketing. From the available evidence, it is difficult to generalise about the extent to which many or most British firms now assume that the product will sell itself. But it is possible to show that the problem of market limitations is an increasingly serious one in many sectors and that many British firms are no more successful than Austin Rover at overcoming market limitations. This point is worth developing because it casts doubt on the premise that the problems of the enterprise can be solved by management at the level of the enterprise.

A great deal of international trade now takes the form of an interchange of manufactures between advanced countries and this is especially so in Western Europe. In this respect, Britain's position is not unusual; by 1980 nearly two-thirds of Britain's manufactured imports came from Western Europe and more than half of our manufactured exports went to Western Europe (Williams *et al.*, 1983, pp. 112–5). The neo-Keynesian advocates of coordinated European reflation would no doubt argue, and with some force, that the prosperity of all the countries in this trading bloc is constrained by a quantitative deficiency of aggregate demand. But for many British manufacturers it is the quality or composition of demand which is the more urgent problem. The growth in interchange of manufactured goods has been associated with a fragmentation of demand as the importers claim an increased share of each national market. Consider, for example, the case of the British white goods market (washing machines, vacuum cleaners, irons and toasters, and so on) which was once dominated by a handful of 'British' firms (Hoover, Hotpoint, Electrolux and Morphy Richards). In all these product lines over the past twenty years, as the importers moved in, the number of brands available increased dramatically, and some importers have deliberately proliferated variant product types as a means of winning market share. This strategy is partly made possible by the emergence of more flexible manufacturing techniques. The combination of this and the fact of fragmentation is sometimes thought to result in a significant tilting of the balance back towards the small producer. No doubt it sometimes does at least lower the long-established advantage of scale. But in most cases success has depended on maintaining volume by holding a sizeable proportion of the home market and selling a small share in a wide range of other countries. In white goods, as in cars, most major producers have lost share of their home market because the dominant firms necessarily lose out in a process of fragmentation; but the successful majors then make good their losses by tipping out small volumes into all or most of the near European markets where they can gain share through the same process.

The problem of British manufacturing is that the managements of major British firms have been unable to win compensating export volume on the scale required. Part of the problem is the very scale that is required. There has not been a simple failure to export. It is more complex than that. As government spokesmen emphasise, British manufacturing as a whole exports a proportion of output which is relatively high in international terms and has been increasing over the past twenty years; in the early 1970s around 25 per cent of British manufacturing output was exported and by the mid-1980s a little over 33 per cent was exported (Williams *et al.*, 1983; Cutler *et al.*, 1986). But this has not benefited the national manufacturing sector because the sector as a whole has been losing home sales faster than it has been increasing export sales. The outward sign of this failure is a growing British balance-of-trade deficit in manufactures, which reached £5.8 billion in 1985 and in recent years has increased at a rate of £1.5 billion a year. This trend is particularly worrying because it is not caused by acute failure in some sectors while others perform satisfactorily; by the trade-balance test, performance in almost all the sectors of British manufacturing is deteriorating.

It is fairly easy to show that the problems are widespread. As part of its evidence to the House of Lords Select Committee on Overseas Trade, the Department of Trade and Industry submitted tables indicating the trends between 1978 and 1983 in import penetration, export performance and balance of payments for the twenty-one Standard Industrial Classification (SIC) 'classes' which at two-digit levels make up manufacturing industry (House of Lords Select Committee on Overseas Trade, 1984–5, Department of Trade memo). The results are summarised in Table 5.1 below. On the positive side they show that, from 1978 to 1983, ten of the twenty-one classes managed an increase in export sales ratio and the pattern in the remaining sectors was usually one of modest fall. Against this reasonably sound achievement on the exports side, there was an overwhelming increase in import penetration, which increased in eighteen classes and these increases were often substantial. Thus, in net terms, only two industrial classes managed an increasing trade surplus and only one sector managed a real increase in trade surplus. In eighteen classes, the trade balance is deteriorating because home market losses are greater than export gains. On this classification, the class which includes cars (motor vehicles and parts) simply represents an extreme version of what has become a general trend. Motor vehicles and parts shows a very slight decline in the export ratio (from 38 to 37 per cent) a substantial increase in the ratio of imports to home demand (35 to 51 per cent) and a balance-of-payments deterioration of nearly £3 billion (£2,874 million). No other class shows anything like the same level of decline (although the trade balance for electrical and electronic engineering worsened by just over £1.5 billion). But nearly all classes are headed in the same direction which means that the home market, essential for volume output, is being lost more rapidly than export markets are being won.

After the Second World War the slogan was 'export or die'. The predicament of British manufacturing in the 1980s under pressure of market fragmentation at home is 'export and die'. Without compensating export sales, white and brown goods firms like Hoover, Hotpoint and Ferguson are being damaged just like Austin Rover in cars. It is also more or less certain that these adverse trends will continue; the fact is that the balance between home and export sales has shifted disastrously and spontaneous recovery now requires a miraculous improvement in the capacity of British manufacturers to make export sales.

In the next section we turn to consider the policy prescriptions which are suggested by our analysis of the Austin Rover experience. If we wish to maintain a viable car manufacturing industry the logic of the situation compels us towards considering some means of safeguarding a larger share of the home market for British manufacturers. It has been argued that the experience of market failure at Austin Rover, though more extreme, fits a widespread pattern in British manufacturing. If so, the conclusion is likely to be similar: if a significant industrial base is to be sustained, some form of political intervention to safeguard the home market in other problem sectors like consumer electronics is essential. More specifically, we now turn to demonstrating the need for a new kind of intervention to safeguard Austin Rover and what remains of British car manufacturing.

Table 5.1. Import penetration, export performance and crude trade balance, by SIC class 1978–83

Class	Ratio A(%)		Ratio B(%)		Export minus imports £m	
	1978	1983	1978	1983	1978	1983
21 Extraction and preparation of metalliferous ores (C)	108	101	391	141	–619	–764
22 Metal manufacturing	25	31	21	25	–236	–672
23 Extraction of minerals NES	32	30	24	24	–252	–140
24 Non-metallic mineral products	9	10	15	11	289	67
25 Chemical industry	28	35	36	41	1192	1578
26 Man-made fibres production	41	68	49	71	82	54
31 Metal goods NES	10	13	13	12	259	–70
32 Mechanical engineering	32	33	44	41	2345	1964
33 Office machinery and data processing equipment (C)	92	109	90	114	–213	–949
34 Electrical and electronic engineering	31	43	37	38	697	–974
35 Motor vehicles and their parts	35	51	38	37	334	–2540
36 Other transport equipment	41	42	45	55	521	1143
37 Instrument engineering	52	56	51	52	–35	–183
41/42 Food, drink and tobacco	18	17	11	11	–1947	–2567
43 Textile industry	31	41	27	28	–270	–1059
44 Leather and leather goods	34	44	26	33	–55	–97
45 Footwear and clothing industries	26	34	18	18	–318	–1020
46 Timber and wooden furniture	27	31	7	5	–896	–1664
47 Paper, printing and publishing	19	20	11	10	–775	–1509
48 Rubber and plastics processing	18	24	21	22	159	–162
49 Other manufacturing industries	35	49	38	37	–139	–459
Divns 2–4 manufacturing industries (revised definition)	24.9	31.4	25.3	27.0	124	–10057

Source: House of Lords Select Committee on Overseas Trade. Evidence of DTI, Tables 4 and 5 1985

A Imports/ home demand (manufacturers' sales + imports − exports)

B Exports/ sales by UK manufacturers

C The overseas trade figures used in calculating the ratios include imports for re-exports. It is possible for ratios A and B to approach or even exceed 100%

What is to be Done?

Although the Conservative government in the mid-1980s contemplates the decline of British manufacturing with equanimity, there can be no doubt that Britain needs a national manufacturing sector. The relative importance of manufacturing employment and output will continue to decline in all the advanced countries but, as we have argued elsewhere (Cutler *et al.*, 1986, chap. 4) the absolute decline of manufacturing in Britain must be resisted because services cannot make the same contribution to either the domestic or the external economy. However it is necessary to be more cautious about arguing the case for the defence of a particular manufacturing industry like motor cars because manufacturing in all the advanced economies renews itself when new, expanding sectors replace old, declining sectors.

Since 1945 the British car industry has been an important part of the national manufacturing sector. In the early 1970s it accounted for 7.3 per cent of total male employment in manufacturing; contributed substantially to the trade balance; and was responsible for 12.3 per cent of the share of manufactures in total national income (Dept of Employment, 1970, Table 82; Central Statistical Office, 1972, Table 18; Dept of Trade, 1979). It is also true that, since the early 1970s, the British car industry has been in precipitous decline. In simple unit terms, UK car production fell from 1.9 million in 1972 to 0.9 million in 1984. The fall in output is even more severe if the unit figures are adjusted to take account of the increasing import content of the cars made in Britain; on this basis Jones (1985b, p. 31) calculates that output fell from 1.8 million to just 0.7 million. Employment in the motor-car industry fell from 510,000 in 1973 to 282,000 in 1984 (Jones, 1985b, p. 9). As car exports flagged and imports flooded in, the balance of payments (in constant prices) on motor vehicles shifted from a surplus of over £4 billion in 1970 to a deficit of £2 billion in 1984. On cars alone there was a decline from a surplus of £1 billion in 1970 to a deficit of £2.7 billion in 1984. While the academics were defining deindustrialisation in the later 1970s, the car industry was suffering from the disease.

The effects of decline within the car industry were magnified through depressive linkage effects which particularly affected the British components industry which had traditionally supplied 50 per cent of the value of each finished car. There has been a very rapid increase in the proportion of the British components market which is taken by imports; this rose from 30 per cent to 50 per cent in the space of only five years up to 1983 (Bessant *et al.*, 1984, p. 37). Although component manufacturers have made strong efforts to compensate by selling abroad, the traditionally large favourable trade balance has remorselessly dwindled (from £769 million in 1978 to £156 million in 1983). In particular the balance with Europe went into deficit in 1982 and it is difficult to see the trend being reversed (House of Commons, Select Committee on European Community, 1983–4, evidence of SMMT). It is unrealistic to imagine that, as domestic demand dwindles, Lucas can go into the West German market with direct exports and sell successfully against Bosch, with its advantages of large scale and close linkages with domestic manufacturers. As firms like Lucas and GKN have long recognised, if British component manufacturers want to tackle West German, French or Italian markets, direct manufacture in these countries is the only way in. Inevitably, such overseas manufacture displaces exports, output and employment from Britain.

The decline of the British car industry is an event, or process, of considerable economic importance. It is especially worrying because it does not seem to be part of any necessary structural shift which makes space for newer, growing industries. The resources released by British industrial decline over the past decade have manifestly not been redeployed into more profitable and efficient uses. This is partly because new industries like information technology are underdeveloped and performing badly in Britain (Cutler *et al.*, 1986). In any case, there is no good structural reason why car manufacturing should migrate from Britain. The UK was in 1983 the western world's fifth largest market and there has been no shift, for example, in factor availability of the sort which would make Britain an inherently inferior location for car production. In all the advanced countries there are currently problems of overcapacity and low profits in the car industry. But none of the other advanced manufacturing countries — Japan, the United States, West Germany, France, Italy — show any sign of moving away from this central activity. The MIT International Automobile Program, looking into the future of the automobile, concluded that car manufacture would not migrate to the newly industrialised countries and predicted that advanced-country producers would dominate the world industry into the twenty-first century (Altshuler *et al.*, 1984). The present situation is that the car industry is declining in Britain but not in the other advanced countries. This is especially unfortunate because it makes it more difficult for Britain to sustain any kind of national presence in the new high-technology industries which rely on the customer base that older domestic industries provide in the advanced countries; in most advanced countries, for example, 50 per cent of the industrial robots are employed in car factories.

If the decline of the British car industry is to be reversed through new policies, it is necessary to be clear about the objectives of such policies. The importance of being clear about objectives was emphasised by the nature of public reaction in the spring of 1986 when the government had been talking with Ford about whether that company would buy Austin Rover and was negotiating with GM about the terms under which that company would buy Leyland trucks and Land Rover. The government then had to back down and break off the negotiations because of chauvinistic criticism from the Left as well as the Right. The tone of the debate was set by Roy Hattersley, who first disclosed the government's sale plans, claiming that Austin Rover was being 'touted to three foreign powers by the Tory government'. The deputy leader of the Labour Party then went on to argue that 'If its plan succeeds there will, by the time of the next general election, be no British motor manufacturer. All of our principal national competitors — West Germany, Italy, Sweden, France, Japan and the United States — will have a national motor industry, but in Britain cars, trucks and buses will be built by wholly owned subsidiaries of foreign firms' (*Financial Times*, 3 February 1986). From this point of view, no self-respecting industrial power allows foreign ownership of its motor industry; we would be going naked into the conference chambers of the economic and financial world if we did not have an independent Austin Rover.

Against such straightforward chauvinism, it is necessary to assert that new policies to reverse the decline of British car manufacture are required so that we can recapture the benefits which the industry used to bring to the economy. More specifically, the aim must be threefold. First, to preserve an important source of employment. At a time when most new jobs created in the economy are for part-time, low-paid female labour, the car industry, with its demand for relatively highly-paid, full-time male employees is especially important. Second, to ensure that most of the value added generated by the industry will accrue to the domestic economy. Any policy should ensure that the main economic benefits of manufacturing cars in Britain are reaped within Britain. And finally, the policy should contribute to stemming the trade deficit on cars, a deficit which has emerged recently, rapidly and hugely.

Set in the context of these objectives, complaints about foreign ownership of British car firms do have some justification. The sourcing decisions of Ford and Vauxhall have led to the import of large numbers of finished cars from their parents' continental European factories while Vauxhall has demoted its British plants from manufacture to assembly of kits which come from German factories. In value added, employment and payments terms, these policies have been disastrous for the British economy. Tied imports ensured that the British content of all Ford cars sold in the United Kingdom in 1984 had fallen to 46 per cent and tied imports plus kit car assembly ensured that the UK content of all GM/Vauxhall cars sold in the UK in 1984 was only 22 per cent (Jones, 1985b, p. 7). On the other hand it is wrong to attribute the decline of the British car industry to the sourcing decisions of the multinationals. The output of the UK car industry fell by nearly a million between the early 1970s and the mid-1980s; the multinational majors accounted for half this fall in output and BL accounted for the other half (Jones, 1985b, p. 4). What we need are new policies which change the market conditions that have forced Austin Rover into retreat and which simultaneously provide an incentive for the multinationals to change their sourcing strategies. If such policies were introduced, the question of foreign ownership of Ford and Vauxhall (or Austin Rover) would cease to be the major issue.

If we need a policy for the car industry, one of the problems of the Thatcher government's approach is that it is more or less exclusively preoccupied with the problems of the one car firm, Austin Rover, which it happens to own. There are two main options for Austin Rover on the government's current agenda. The first option is a policy of benign neglect which leaves Austin Rover in the public sector as a state-owned car company. Under the terms of the current BL five-year plan, finally agreed in June 1985, the government will not provide any more public funding for Austin Rover. On this scenario, the present management is left to carry on as best it can, mainly by developing the collaboration with Honda. No doubt because it is unlikely that the company can survive without making further calls on state funding, the government has actively pursued its second option of privatisation which involves the sale of Austin Rover, like other Rover Group divisions, to a private company. In effect, on this second option, the old state company of BL (now Rover Group) is liquidated; the state writes off £2,100 million of state capital which has been injected since 1977 and the state pays out on the £1,500 million of state guarantees on the company's private borrowings which the new owners of Rover Group will not take over. The cost of this kind of liquidation/privatisation is high but at least it puts an end to the state's open-ended commitment. In our view, however, neither of the government's options is attractive or sensible because they fail all the necessary criteria: that is, they are unlikely to maintain or increase domestic value added, employment and yield a payments surplus.

The stark problem with any policy of leaving Austin Rover as an independent car company is that it is difficult to see how the company can survive as a manufacturer of motor cars. The logic of the situation drives the company towards assembly of another manufacturer's models. As an unprofitable company, Austin Rover cannot now finance the independent development of new models. Even if such models were to be developed, market limitations at home and abroad ensure low model volume which would prevent the company manufacturing cars profitably or recouping development costs. The only way out is for Austin Rover to cooperate as a junior partner with a fully-fledged car manufacturer. The present management has accepted the inevitable and adopted a strategy of assembling Hondas. The first result was the Rover 800, launched in the summer of 1986. After this, all the company's present models will be replaced one by one with badge-engineered Hondas. The negative results in terms of diminished value added and employment are obvious and will probably outweigh any payments benefits which arise, if Honda keeps its word, and allows the company to assemble 100,000 cars a year for sale through Honda's European dealer network. It is important to emphasise that these negative results cannot now be avoided by putting in more state money. Generally, state funding would allow the company to develop another generation of its own new models. But, as long as the market is limited, there is no prospect of obtaining a return on such investment.

If the *de facto* subordination of Austin Rover to another manufacturer is inevitable under present market conditions, the results would not be much better if the government enforced a *de jure* subordination through privatisation and sold the company off to another car manufacturer. The first problem with this option is finding a purchaser who wants to buy a small, non-specialist car producer with low model volumes, substantial overcapacity and rickety finances. Against this, however, Austin Rover has a well-developed distribution network in Britain and holds an 18 per cent share of that market, which is the third largest for cars in Europe. From this point of view, the obvious purchaser was Ford. In marketing terms, the purchase of Austin Rover was an attractive defensive move because it would buttress Ford's share of the British market where it is under acute pressure from GM/Vauxhall. Defence of market leadership in Britain is of some importance to Ford of Europe because Britain is the only national market in Europe where Ford is car market leader and it is also the national market where Ford has traditionally earned its profits; in the German market Ford's Escort model claims just 4 per cent of the market. Chauvinist reaction has, however, effectively vetoed a deal with Ford, so Honda emerges as the next most likely purchaser. Through buying Austin Rover, Honda would gain British market share, would secure a collaboration which must end if any other manufacturer buys Austin Rover and would obtain control of the British factories so that Japanese-style management could be put on to the essential job of improving the quality of a product which, under the present five-year plan, will be partly sold under the Honda badge. In many ways, however, this kind of speculation about the motives and identity of the purchasing company is irrelevant because the outcome in terms of British value added and employment will be much the same whoever buys Austin Rover.

The broad terms of the deal with the British government will be much the same whatever the identity of the purchaser. The government will have to offer to write off the accumulated debts of Austin Rover which now stand at £1,500 million; no purchaser will be prepared to take over this liability. For internal political consumption, the government will also need to insist on an understanding about the level of British content in Austin Rover car output and perhaps also about employment in the cars division. There must be a substantial question mark over the value of such undertakings; the precedent of Chrysler's 1975 'declaration of intent' about the future of its UK operations is not very reassuring because that declaration (like the subsequent planning agreement) did not prevent the run-down of car manufacturing by Chrysler in Britain or the subsequent sale of the British operation to Peugeot (Wilks, 1984, pp. 252–65, 297–8). Furthermore, if the government's main priority is the privatisation of Austin Rover, it is hardly in a position to stand out for terms which would effectively tie the purchaser. However well intentioned the purchaser is, Austin Rover under new ownership must face the same market limits which ensure that its financial and productive performance will remain inferior. Within these market limits, manufacture cannot be profitable, so the future has to be assembly with the Austin Rover factories annexed to a larger strategy of multinational manufacture. Cynically, the main advantage of disposal is political; the burden of responsibility for unpalatable decisions about employment and content levels would be transferred on to a foreign company.

The unattractive (even unacceptable) consequences of the policy options on the government's agenda in the mid-1980s are inevitable because these policies do not confront the market limitations which have motored Austin Rover's decline. Whether the company is sold off or not, as long as the market limitations are not shifted, whoever runs Austin Rover will have no option but to take out manufacturing capacity and shed workers as the company retreats into assembly. Until the inward flood of imports is stemmed by government policy, the enterprise managers at Austin Rover (and other firms in a similar predicament) must pursue a strategy of following the market down. It is significant that, in the first half of 1986, the government faced three industrial policy crises about Westland, BL and British Shipbuilders. All three crises were about firms with empty order books or with much more capacity than orders. Westland was a special case because here there was a temporary failure of the military demand which normally shelters British weapons producers. BL and BS were more typical in that their crises were caused by a failure to reserve a larger share of British civil demand. The long-term consequences of following the market down are clearest in shipbuilding. Throughout the 1950s, the British shipbuilding industry employed more than 200,000 workers on civil and warship construction; by spring 1986 the remaining civil yards employed less than 10,000, and British Shipbuilders management have proposed further closures which will reduce the work-force to nearer 5,000. Austin Rover workers obviously have some grounds for apprehension arising from the spring 1986 decision of the government to install as chairman of BL, Mr Graham Day, the chief executive who led British Shipbuilders while it followed the market down towards insignificance. The company seems likely to proceed with closures and redundancies which will be presented as regrettably necessary because there is no alternative.

But in our view there *is* an alternative which could at least soften the blow of the next round of closures and sackings at Austin Rover. Any radical solution must shift the market limits by reserving a larger share of British demand for domestic manufacturers. The question is, how should this be done? In the case of cars we would suggest that various forms of tax privilege should be offered to companies (and maybe also private individuals) who buy and run British manufactured cars which have a British value added content of 80 per cent or more. In the company car market, which accounts for more than 60 per cent of new car sales, it would be possible to offer car tax rebates on British manufactured cars. The use of such cars could be encouraged by differential rates of vehicle excise duty and income tax penalties for users of non-British company cars. Central government departments, local councils and nationalised industries could be directed to review their purchasing policies and buy British whenever possible. The administrative details of a system of value added content regulation are not very important at this stage. What we wish to do here is simply to argue the case for a new principle of preference for the British manufactured product. In our view this is essential if employment and value added are to be maintained in the British industry. We also wish to change the terms of the debate about the car industry in Britain. We are convinced that the debate about who owns the British car industry is a bogus one; if the correct policies of safeguarding the market for British manufactured cars are adopted, the question of public or private and native or foreign ownership becomes a secondary one.

As the leading manufacturer of British cars, Austin Rover would be the main beneficiary of new policies of value added content regulation. But what we are proposing is a constructive policy for defending the remnant of the British car manufacturing industry before it ceases to exist. Under current market conditions, a dispersed car assembly industry is now emerging in Britain. One of the three majors, Vauxhall is already merely an assembler of half-British motor cars. And the Japanese are actually being enticed into the assembly game which various European firms like Peugeot are already playing in their British factories. But there still exist two firms producing volume cars (Austin Rover and Ford), and they have four factories (Longbridge, Cowley, Dagenham and Halewood) which can each produce cars with an 80 per cent British content. All these factories have been completely re-equipped and retooled in the period since 1979. Something like £1,500 million of taxpayer's money has been invested in Austin Rover, while Ford spent £1,650 million between 1979 and 1983 on its car production facilities (Jones, 1985b, p. 9). Moreover, these facilities for manufacturing cars have a capacity of around 1.2 million cars and have been substantially underutilised in recent years; Austin Rover and Ford jointly have excess capacity for some 600,000 cars divided roughly equally between the two firms (*Financial Times*, 12 January 1985; Jones, 1985b, p. 22). A policy, such as we suggest, of encouraging domestic manufacture would load these factories with throughput generating domestic employment and value added in the car firms and in the failing car components industry. Our policies would also promote the renewal of the industry through the orderly admission of new entrants who would have an incentive to undertake licensed manufacture rather than kit car assembly. Even with safeguarding, the financing of both development and manufacturing will be difficult for a relatively small firm (like Austin Rover). But safeguarding the home market could allow much of the heavy, but crucial, development costs to be reduced through licensing from larger foreign firms. Moreover, in particular, the form of value added content regulation which we propose would put the pressure on Nissan to move beyond a small-scale assembly operation which on current plans will only expand to produce 100,000 cars a year.

Policies of preference for British-manufactured cars meet our urgent need to defend and develop the country's existing car manufacturing base. It would be idle to pretend that the implementation of such a policy would not be fraught with difficulties. We cannot remove the threat to the British car industry from Japan and Europe without offending anyone. But, if the new policies were politically presented in the right way, it should be possible to avoid massive retaliation against British exports. And there is no reason why moderate protective action on one commodity (or a few commodities) by a minor industrial power should threaten the current system of international trade.

The responses of Japan and Europe represent problems of a different order. The British government has long relied on import quotas as a means of limiting imports of cars from Japan: by a voluntary agreement the Japanese are restricted to 11 per cent of the British market. Our agreement on cars with Japan is a bilateral one and could be renegotiated to impose more stringent limitations on the French pattern, or exclusion on the Italian pattern. The size of our overall trade deficit with Japan justifies such an approach and the imbalance is such that Japanese retaliation against British exports is not a problem. To the extent that imports of built-up cars from Japan are reduced, that would make more room on the British market for European-manufactured cars. This is important because the aim has to be to introduce some safeguarding measures which are in breach of EEC rules without alienating the other members of the EEC to the extent that they retaliate or expel us from the club. At this point the nature of the measures and their effects on mainland European producers becomes crucial. The new policies we propose would aim to safeguard the national market rather than protect the British producers by excluding all the European majors. Safeguarding would not prevent manufacturers like VW or Renault from continuing to make low volume sales to private buyers and thereby taking their normal 5 per cent share of the fragmented British market. The policy we propose has two modest aims, neither of which is violently anti-European. The first aim is to give the national major (Austin Rover) a share of its home market which is similar to that held by Renault in France or VW in Germany. The second aim is to discourage the two other 'British' majors (Ford and GM) from operating sourcing policies under which both import large numbers of built-up cars into the UK and one brings in kits for assembly. Our proposals could give Austin Rover up to 30 per cent of the home market and would induce Ford to source in Britain. That matters greatly to the British economy. But, in a broader European perspective, these limited new measures and their results would fall far short of representing a massive threat to the Treaty of Rome of a kind which required a major reaction.

We shall be attacked for encouraging the kind of economic chauvinism about which we were earlier so disdainful, and for fostering inefficiency. But we are not here insisting that particular firms have to be wrapped in the flag. Ford would be a crucial component of the home manufacture industry and, as we have noted, ownership of Austin Rover or Ford is not the main issue. The concern is with value added, employment and the trade balance. These are all crucial aspects of a healthy and viable British economy which is essential for all our futures. Nor will there be any shortage of competition or choice, for buyers will be able to choose from amongst the British models and from continuing imports. The aim of our proposal is to control an unstructured and excessive competition in the British car market which prevents Austin Rover and Ford's factories from working efficiently and which more generally undermines the continuance of car manufacture. Above all, those who doubt the wisdom of our proposals should consider two points. First, what we propose covers just one manufactured commodity and the proposal is for preference rather than full protection, safeguarding rather than exclusion. It may be that similarly limited and cautious policies might be usefully examined for a small range of other problem areas, such as consumer electronics and data processing, but that is not the immediate concern. Second, the risks entailed in our policy should be judged against the certainty of further damaging decline in manufacturing if present trends and policies continue.

In this respect it is interesting to note that there is now an increasing convergence of opinion on the current crisis between academics like ourselves and leading industrialists like John Harvey-Jones and Lord Weinstock. Thus, when Lord Weinstock appeared before the House of Lords Select Committee on Overseas Trade, he succintly made a point with which it is easy to agree: 'British industry may be bad in many ways . . . let us assume we are very bad. But so long as we exist we can be improved. If you make Government policy so as to crush us, we will not be there' (House of Lords Select Committee on Overseas Trade, 1984–85, Evidence Q. 1394). How long will it be before middle-of-the-road opinion in Britain catches up with these shared perceptions? And how much longer will it be before the political resistances inside all the major parties are overcome to the extent that such new policy initiatives can at least be openly discussed, if not implemented? This last question is of crucial importance. After the Austin Rover experiment in changing management culture has failed, one overriding lesson seems to stand out from the present survey: at this late stage Britain's future as a car manufacturing nation depends on a change of political culture.

Appendix A / Accounting for Austin Rover

The control of operating losses was an important priority for the Edwardes team. This objective was of considerable political importance when so much emphasis is placed on the bottom-line profit and loss figure as a measure of enterprise success and failure in the nationalised industries. Our book has demonstrated that the post-1977 'recovery strategy' failed and the discussion in Chapter 4 on investment strategy implies that Austin Rover was inherently unprofitable as a car manufacturer. But paradoxically, as Table A.1 shows, Austin Rover's operating losses were controlled in the years 1983–5 even as the strategy was not working. BL Cars division (including Austin Rover) made its worst-ever trading loss of £271 million in 1980. But it was then turned round financially so that by 1983 there was a small trading profit of just £3 million; the 1984 and 1985 results, with losses of £24 million and £10 million, were worse but not much worse. The paradox of improved financial results amidst strategic failure can be resolved if we remember that financial results can be improved in one of two ways: an enterprise can control operating losses by solving the market and productive problems of the business; or, alternatively, an enterprise can control operating losses by financial adjustments within the framework of the accounting conventions. When the strategy was not delivering the necessary sales revenue the management team could only produce improved financial results by the latter route. It should be emphasised that these financial adjustments were perfectly legal and proper; management has the right to represent any enterprise's financial results as it thinks best within the prevailing accounting conventions. But at the same time, management should not complain about the fair comment that financial adjustments can produce profit and loss figures which reflect a markedly optimistic view of the viability of the enterprise.

It is extraordinarily difficult to follow the financial progress of Austin Rover over the past decade from the published annual reports and accounts which are filed in Companies House. Austin

Rover was created by corporate reorganisation at the beginning of the 1980s and its published accounts only cover the years from 1982 onwards. BL and Austin Rover have never published any kind of five- or ten-year historical summary which relates the ARG results to those of the same businesses when they were part of the larger BL Cars division. This is an issue of some importance because without comparable statistics and a historical summary, outsiders must remain perplexed and puzzled about a number of points. For example, when BL Cars division was broken up, Austin Rover 'inherited' a revenue deficit of £751.8 million which was 80 per cent of the revenue deficit of the previous BL Cars group. Without a historical summary, we are unable to decide whether this is a fair reflection of Austin Morris's contribution to the huge revenue deficit or whether the 80 per cent ratio was simply an arbitrary book-keeper's decision. It is also true that anyone who consults the Austin Rover report, which is filed with the division's accounts, will find that it is a pretty thin document. The report contains few statements of strategy and none of the supporting exhibits which a large public company would normally provide. For example, sales breakdowns by product and geographical market have never been provided. Neither the report nor the accounts contain the information which city analysts and investment managers would normally expect from a major public company. The British taxpayers who have financed BL for more than ten years have never been given this information. And, if the members of the public wish to know more they are best advised to find a friendly Member of Parliament; BL's strategy plans (minus 'commercially sensitive information') are filed in the House of Commons library which can only be used by MPs.

All this seems surprisingly secretive behaviour for a major state enterprise which we all own. Nevertheless, if we are interested in the use of the accounting conventions in order to improve profitability, the fundamentals are fairly clear from the published accounts. Ordinary (pre- and post-tax) profit is a residual which appears after the deduction of depreciation and interest payments; if depreciation and interest payments are lower then the operating profit will be greater. The treatment of depreciation and the management of interest charges were crucial to the control of operating losses. Austin Rover has maintained the appearance of financial viability by making modest depreciation provision. The division is also helped by a peculiar arrangement with its parent holding company, BL PLC, which provides a funding framework that keeps the interest burden low. The company has also benefited from the

Table A.1. Austin Rover Group financial performance, 1977–84

	1984	1983	1982	1981	1980	1979	1978	1977
Turnover £m	1849.7	1799.4	1582.3	1840.2	1910.5	1989.3	2232.1	1992.1
Trading (loss)/profit	(23.7)	2.7	(105.9)	(178.9)	(270.7)	(58.2)	42.4	35.5
Manpower reduction £m	–	–	–	–	–	9.7	9.5	–
Interest payable £m	(20.6)	(19.0)	(28.3)	(32.0)	(58.3)	(34.0)	(56.7)	(50.8)
Profit/loss on ordinary activities	(44.3)	(16.3)	(134.2)	(210.9)	(329.0)	(101.9)	(23.8)	(15.3)
Tax recovered	20.6	8.9	–	–	–	–	–	–
Tax paid	–	–	0.2	0.2	0.1	0.2	0.2	0.3
Loss after tax £m	(23.7)	(7.4)	(134.4)	(211.1)	(329.1)	(102.1)	(24.0)	(15.6)

Table A.1 *continued*

Minority share of profits of subsidiary	(1.5)	(1.7)	(2.2)	-	-	-	-	-
Extra-ordinary items	2.7	0.7	(37.8)	(103.0)	(84.9)	(7.8)	(4.2)	(23.5)
Loss after extra-ordinary items £m	(22.5)	(9.6)	(174.4)	(314.1)	(414.0)	(109.9)	(28.2)	(39.1)
Accumulated deficit at start of year £m	(936.0)	(926.2)	(751.8)	(617.5)	(203.5)	(93.6)	(65.4)	(26.3)
Loss during year	(24.5)	(9.8)	(174.4)	(314.1)	(414.0)	(109.9)	(28.2)	(39.1)
Accumulated deficit at year end £m	(960.5)	(936.0)	(926.2)	(931.6)	(617.5)	(203.5)	(93.6)	(65.4)

Source: See Table A.2.
Notes: See Table A.2.

accounting convention that the costs of plant closure are treated as 'extraordinary costs'; these costs are entered in the accounts as a charge below the bottom line profit figure and therefore do not increase the division's reported losses.

Some nationalised enterprises, like the Central Electricity Generating Board, make depreciation provision on a modern equivalent replacement (MER) cost basis. They do more than make depreciation provision for replacing their existing capital equipment with similar plant at current prices; their depreciation provision covers the cost of buying in the next generation of capital equipment which is more sophisticated and expensive than the plant currently in use. If Austin Rover wants to stay in a manufacturing business where techniques are changing, it would be sensible to make this kind of MER depreciation provision; at a guess, this kind of depreciation provision would at least double the present depreciation charge and this would increase the operating losses by £100 million. As it is, Austin Rover makes a modest historic cost depreciation provision on the original (pre-inflation) cost of that part of its capital equipment which is not fully depreciated and this charge amounted to £87 million in 1983 and £71 million in 1984. This historic charge does not reflect what it would cost to buy in similar equipment at current (post-inflation) prices nor does it make any provision for replacing fully-depreciated equipment which is still in use. A number of other indications suggest that the company is concerned to take a low depreciation figure within the historic cost framework. In 1984 Austin Rover changed its depreciation policy by extending the write-off period for certain plant and tooling, and this reduced operating losses by some £15 million. More recently, BL has resisted proposals that fully depreciated assets be taken back on to the balance sheet and redepreciated. The decision to take a low depreciation allowance is within management's prerogative, but we would suggest that Austin Rover's management is behaving shortsightedly when depreciation provides a source of finance for new investment; low depreciation allowances improve current financial losses at the expense of limiting the internal fund available to finance investment. This decision now threatens to create a crisis because, under the five-year plan approved in June 1985, BL (and Austin Rover) will not receive any more investment funds from the state. When Austin Rover is making losses and taking low depreciation payments, we cannot see how the plans for the car division can be financed from internal funds.

Some nationalised enterprises like British Coal are crippled by

Table A.2. Cars division:[1] loans and fixed assets, 1977–84

	Loans (£m)	Gross fixed assets[5] (£m)	Sales Revenue (at 1980 prices)[6] (£m)
1977	350.0[2]	607.3	2,771
1978	519.6[3]	736.5	2,821
1979	789.7[3]	888.1	2,255
1980	1,061.6[3]	1,036.3	1,911
1981	1,486.5[3]	1,079.3	1,781
1982	1,079.0[4]	1,172.4	1,439
1983	1,196.2[4]	1,254.1	1,534
1984	1,236.4[4]	1,150.0	1,480

Source: BL Cars and Austin Rover Group accounts.

1. BL Cars 1977–81: Austin Rover 1982–4.
2. Parent company loans.
3. Group company loans.
4. Holding company loans from BL plc to Austin Rover Group.
5. Plant and machinery employed at cost plus additions minus disposals.
6. BL Cars division to 1981, then Austin Rover Group.

interest charges and unable to earn a profit because their strategic investment has been financed by loans at high rates of interest from the government. Austin Rover is in a more fortunate position because its interest charges are very low; as Table A.1 shows, these interest charges used to cost the BL cars division £50 million or more but they have been reduced and now cost Austin Rover just £20 million in recent years. In the Austin Rover accounts interest charges appear to cover only the cost of short-term borrowing which provides working capital requirements; they are the financial costs of holding stocks and work in progress. This is rather peculiar because the parent holding company has huge borrowings on which it pays large sums of interest; BL (plc) has obtained £2,100 million of interest-free public dividend capital from the state but it has also borrowed some £1,500 million from private sources. The parent company's funding is therefore half in the form of public equity and half in the form of private loans. This funding has been applied in the operating divisions which make cars and trucks and much has been used to purchase fixed capital equipment. Table A.2 shows that, as fixed assets in the cars division increased after 1977, so did loans from the parent holding company. But, in the case of Austin Rover, the parent company's funds are passed on in the form of loans on which the operating division pays no interest at all; by 1984, the operating division had drawn £1,300 million in interest free loans from the parent holding company. By this means, the operating results of the division are substantially improved because the costs of the loans which have funded nearly half Austin Rover's capital requirement are carried entirely in the accounts of the parent holding company.

Our discussion of Austin Rover's financial results must finally consider how the division benefited from the accounting conventions about 'extraordinary items'. A retreating enterprise which closes peripheral plants incurs substantial costs because it must write off assets and pay off redundant workers. In the Austin Rover accounts, these costs are classified as 'extraordinary items' and they amounted to no less than £225 million in the three years from 1980 to 1982. But these costs did not reduce profits because, under current accounting conventions, the charge for extraordinary items is entered in the accounts after the profit (or loss) on ordinary activities has been calculated; the presentation of financial results in Table A.1 above shows this. Thus while the company was successfully controlling losses in the years 1980 to 1982, large costs were being incurred below the bottom-line profit and loss figure. These costs increased an accumulating revenue deficit which was not covered by sales revenue because, as Table A.2 shows, in real terms sales revenue was completely flat. As Table A.1 shows, this revenue deficit grew rapidly in the late 1970s, and from 1981 onwards was running at between £900 and £1,000 million. The revenue deficit has only been contained at this level by the various arrangements for minimising divisional costs which keep depreciation and interest charges at a very low level. In many ways, in a nationalised enterprise which has run up huge losses, the accumulated revenue deficit is a much better measure of strategic performance than the bottom-line profit and loss figure. There can be no doubt that by this financial standard, the strategy has failed.

Appendix B / Production and Market Statistics

Table B.1. Company shares of UK new car market

	New car registrations (000s)	British Leyland (%)	Ford (%)	Vauxhall (%)	Others (%)
1970	1126.8	38.1	26.5	10.0	25.4
1971	1334.7	40.2	18.7	10.7	30.4
1972	1702.2	33.1	24.5	8.9	33.5
1973	1688.3	31.8	22.6	8.0	37.6
1974	1273.8	32.7	22.7	7.3	37.3
1975	1211.7	30.8	21.7	7.4	40.1
1976	1307.9	27.4	25.2	8.9	38.5
1977	1335.3	24.3	25.7	9.1	40.9
1978	1618.2	23.5	24.7	8.2	43.6
1979	1731.9	19.6	28.3	8.2	43.9
1980	1513.8	18.2	30.7	8.8	42.3
1981	1484.7	19.2	30.9	8.6	41.3
1982	1555.0	17.8	30.5	11.7	40.0
1983	1791.7	18.6	28.9	14.6	37.9
1984	1749.7	17.8	27.8	16.1	38.3
1985	1832.4	17.9	26.5	16.6	39.0

Source: Society of Motor Manufacturers and Traders, *Annual Statistics*, various years.

Table B.2. British Leyland[1] production, exports and share of new car registrations, 1970–85

	Production of cars (000s)	Exports of cars (000s)	Total UK car sales (000s)	BL home car sales (000s)	UK marke share (%
1970	788.7	368.4	1076.9	410.4	38.1
1971	868.7	385.8	1285.6	516.3	40.2
1972	916.2	347.3	1637.8	542.4	33.1
1973	875.8	348.0	1661.4	529.6	31.8
1974	738.5	322.5	1268.8	415.4	32.7
1975	605.1	256.7	1194.1	368.7	30.8
1976	687.9	320.8	1285.6	352.7	27.4
1977	651.0	293.3	1323.5	322.1	24.3
1978	611.6	247.9	1591.9	373.8	23.5
1979	503.8	200.2	1716.3	337.0	19.6
1980	395.8	157.8	1513.8	275.8	18.2
1981	413.4	126.2	1484.7	285.1	19.2
1982	405.1	133.9	1555.0	277.3	17.8
1983	473.3	118.3	1791.7	332.7	18.6
1984	383.3	78.6	1749.7	312.1	17.8
1985	465.1	n/a	1832.4	328.0	17.9

Source: as Table B.1.

1. Total includes Austin Rover, Jaguar/Daimler and Range Rover.

Table B.3. Austin Morris/Austin Rover production, exports and share of new car registrations, 1970–85

	Production of cars (000s)	Export allocation (000s)	Total UK car sales (000s)	Austin home sales (000s)	UK market share (%)
1970	588.0	279.4	1076.9	309.0	28.7
1971	665.9	301.2	1285.6	380.3	29.6
1972	697.7	274.5	1637.8	406.6	24.8
1973	672.5	270.1	1661.4	397.9	23.9
1974	561.0	248.7	1268.8	355.9	28.0
1975	449.9	172.3	1194.1	291.7	24.4
1976	–	–	1285.6	280.2	21.7
1977	–	–	1323.5	245.5	18.5
1978	612.0	248.0	1591.9	374.0	23.4
1979	504.0	200.0	1716.3	337.0	19.6
1980	396.0	158.0	1513.8	270.0	17.8
1981	413.0	126.0	1484.7	280.0	18.8
1982	405.0	134.0	1555.0	277.0	17.8
1983	473.0	118.0	1791.7	326.0	18.2
1984	383.0	85.0	1750.0	312.0	17.8
1985	465.0	–	1832.0	328.0	17.9

Source: as Table B.1.

Note: Figures before 1982 apply to Austin Morris, and after 1982 to Austin Rover. Triumph is included throughout. Production and export allocation figures for 1978–83 include Jaguar.

Table B.4. Fragmentation of sales in major UK market classes

(a) Small car class

	1965	1966	1967	1968	1969	1970	1971	1972	197
Ford Fiesta	-	-	-	-	-	-	-	-	-
Austin Mini	104477 (9.5)	91624 (8.7)	82435 (7.4)	86190 (7.8)	68330 (7.1)	80740 (7.5)	103180 (8.1)	96314 (5.9)	963 (5.
Austin Metro	-	-	-	-	-	-	-	-	-
Vauxhall Nova	-	-	-	-	-	-	-	-	-

(b) Light car class

	1965	1966	1967	1968	1969	1970	1971	1972	19
Ford Escort	-	-	-	98218 (8.9)	85156 (8.8)	95782 (8.9)	89143 (6.9)	140837 (8.6)	11 (6
1100/1300	157679 (14.3)	151146 (14.4)	131383 (11.8)	151146 (13.7)	133455 (13.8)	132965 (12.4)	133527 (10.4)	102449 (6.3)	5 (3
Allegro	-	-	-	-	-	-	-	-	2 (1
Acclaim	-	-	-	-	-	-	-	-	-
Maestro	-	-	-	-	-	-	-	-	-
Vauxhall Viva	58884 (5.3)	59731 (5.7)	100200 (9.0)	101067 (9.1)	75354 (7.8)	76838 (7.1)	92994 (7.2)	99393 (6.0)	9 (5
Vauxhall Astra/ Chevette	-	-	-	-	-	-	-	-	-

continued on pp. 130–1

4	1975	1976	1977	1978	1979	1980	1981	1982	1983	1984
	-	-	40934 (3.1)	68723 (4.3)	58681 (3.4)	91661 (6.1)	110753 (7.5)	110165 (7.2)	119602 (6.7)	125851 (7.2)
82 1)	84688 (7.1)	81107 (6.3)	60337 (4.6)	72617 (4.6)	82938 (4.8)	61129 (4.0)	28772 (1.9)	25503 (1.6)	27739 (1.5)	- -
	-	-	-	-	-	- -	110283 (7.4)	114550 (7.4)	137303 (7.7)	117442 (6.7)
	-	-	-	-	-	-	-	-	24995 (1.4)	55442 (3.2)

4	1975	1976	1977	1978	1979	1980	1981	1982	1983	1984
99 3)	103817 (8.7)	133959 (10.4)	103389 (7.8)	114415 (7.2)	131667 (7.7)	122357 (8.1)	141081 (9.5)	166942 (10.7)	174190 (9.7)	157340 (9.0)
30 6)	-	-	-	-	-	-	-	-	-	-
19 3)	63339 (5.3)	55218 (4.3)	56175 (4.2)	61535 (3.9)	59985 (3.5)	39612 (2.6)	20753 (1.5)	-	-	-
	-	-	-	-	-	-	-	42188 (2.3)	38406 (2.1)	34728 (2.0)
	-	-	-	-	-	-	-	-	65328 (3.6)	83072 (4.7)
52)	54792 (4.6)	33901 (2.6)	17249 (1.4)	-	-	-	-	-	-	-
	19847 (1.7)	43827 (3.4)	51763 (3.9)	52327 (3.3)	44197 (2.6)	46059 (3.0)	36838 (2.5) (1.6)	70254 (4.5) (1.9)	62570 (3.5) (2.1)	56411 (3.2)

Table B.4. *continued*

(c) Medium car class

	1965	1966	1967	1968	1969	1970	1971	1972	1
Ford Cortina	116985 (10.6)	127307 (12.1)	165300 (14.9)	137873 (12.5)	116186 (12.0)	123025 (11.4)	102214 (7.9)	187159 (11.4)	1 (
Ford Sierra	–	–	–	–	–	–	–	–	–
BL Maxi	–	–	34498 (3.1)	30284 (2.7)	30784 (3.2)	36753 (3.4)	42867 (3.3)	53984 (3.3)	
Marina/Ital	–	–	–	–	–	–	41164 (3.2)	104986 (6.4)	1
Dolomite	–	–	–	–	–	–	–	13004 (0.8)	
Montego	–	–	–	–	–	–	–	–	–
Vauxhall Cavalier	–	–	–	–	–	–	–	–	–

Source: as Table B.1.

4	1975	1976	1977	1978	1979	1980	1981	1982	1983	1984
234 .3)	106787 (8.9)	126238 (9.8)	120601 (9.1)	139204 (8.7)	193784 (11.3)	190281 (12.6)	159804 (10.8)	135745 (8.7)	-	-
	-	-	-	-	-	-	-	-	159119 (8.9)	113071 (6.5)
072 .8)	26950 (2.3)	33486 (2.6)	26339 (2.0)	32000 (2.0)	30169 (1.8)	22229 (1.5)	-	-	-	-
.439 .4)	78632 (6.6)	71288 (5.5)	66088 (5.0)	82638 (5.3)	62140 (3.6)	59906 (3.9)	48490 (3.3)	23228 (1.6)	-	-
.008 .5)	30119 (2.6)	30197 (2.3)	24764 (1.9)	-	-	-	-	-	-	-
	-	-	-	-	-	-	-	-	-	-
	373	29762 (2.3)	41128 (3.1)	55373 (3.5)	46517 (2.7)	41119 (2.7)	33631 (2.3)	100081 (6.4)	127509 (7.1)	132149 (7.5)

Table B.5. Top ten best-selling cars in the UK, 1967–85

(a) Top ten by model

Top ten by model and company	1967	1968	1969	1970	1971	1972	1973	1974	19
1	Cortina (F)	1100/1300 (BL)	1100/1300 (BL)	1100/1300 (BL)	1100/1300 (BL)	Cortina (F)	Cortina (F)	Cortina (F)	Co
2	1100/1300 (BL)	Cortina (F)	Cortina (F)	Cortina (F)	Mini (BL)	Escort (F)	Marina (BL)	Escort (F)	Es
3	Viva (V)	Viva (V)	Escort (F)	Escort (F)	Cortina (F)	Marina (BL)	Escort (F)	Mini (BL)	Mi
4	Mini (BL)	Escort (F)	Viva (V)	Mini (BL)	Viva (V)	1100/1300 (BL)	Viva (V)	Marina (BL)	Ma
5	Anglia (F)	Mini (BL)	Mini (BL)	Viva (V)	Escort (F)	Viva (V)	Mini (BL)	Allegro (BL)	Al
6	Minx (C)	Minx (C)	Minx (C)	Avenger (C)	Avenger (C)	Mini (BL)	Avenger (C)	Avenger (C)	Vi
7	Victor (V)	Victor (V)	Husky (C)	Capri (F)	Maxi (BL)	Avenger (C)	Hunter (C)	Dolomite (BL)	A
8	Corsair (F)	Corsair (F)	Maxi (BL)	Maxi (BL)	Hunter (C)	Maxi (BL)	1100/1300 (BL)	Hunter (C)	Do
9	Minor (BL)	Maxi (BL)	Corsair (F)	1800/2200 (BL)	Marina (BL)	Hunter (C)	Dolomite (BL)	Maxi (BL)	Pr
10	Maxi (BL)	Herald (BL)	Victor (V)	Rover (BL)	1800/2200 (BL)	Victor (V)	Maxi (BL)	Princess (BL)	He

(b) Top ten by numbers sold

Rank	1967	1968	1969	1970	1971	1972	1973	1974	1975
1	165300	151146*	133455*	132965*	133527*	187159	181607	131234	106787
2	131382*	137873	116186	123025	103180*	140837	115041*	91699	103817
3	100220	101067	85156	95782	102214	104986*	114296	89686*	84688*
4	82436*	98218	75354	80740*	99393	102449*	97893	81439*	78632*
5	55735	86190*	68330*	76838	89143	99393	96383*	60619*	63339*
6	39903	36999	36094	50133	63476	96314*	78644	60224	54792
7	38517	34772	31014	38346	42867*	78729	65500	45008*	38877
8	35993	31014	30784*	36752*	41996	53984*	59198*	37158*	30119*
9	34565*	30284*	29005*	32927*	41164*	50342	57439*	36072*	29067*
10	34498*	29926*	28688	25233*	39163*	36651	52853*	25335*	28966
Number of BL models in top ten registrations									
	4	4	4	5	5	4	5	6	5

continued on pp. 134–5

1976	1977	1978	1979	1980	1981	1982	1983	1984	1985
Cortina (F)	Cortina (F)	Cortina (F)	Cortina (F)	Cortina (F)	Cortina (F)	Escort (F)	Escort (F)	Escort (F)	Escort (F)
Escort (F)	Escort (F)	Escort (F)	Escort (F)	Escort (F)	Escort (F)	Cortina (F)	Sierra (F)	Cavalier (V)	Cavalier (V)
Mini (BL)	Marina (BL)	Marina (BL)	Mini (BL)	Fiesta (F)	Fiesta (F)	Metro (BL)	Metro (BL)	Fiesta (F)	Fiesta (F)
Marina (BL)	Mini (BL)	Mini (BL)	Marina (BL)	Mini (BL)	Metro (BL)	Fiesta (F)	Cavalier (V)	Metro (BL)	Metro (BL)
Allegro (BL)	Allegro (BL)	Fiesta (F)	Allegro (BL)	Marina (BL)	Ital (BL)	Cavalier (V)	Fiesta (F)	Sierra (F)	Sierra (F)
Chevette (V)	Chevette (V)	Allegro (BL)	Fiesta (F)	Chevette (V)	Chevette (V)	Astra (V)	Maestro (BL)	Maestro (B)	Astra (V)
Viva (V)	Capri (F)	Cavalier (V)	Granada (F)	Cavalier (V)	Cavalier (V)	Acclaim (BL)	Astra (V)	Astra (V)	Montego (BL)
Maxi (BL)	Cavalier (V)	Chevette (V)	Capri (F)	Allegro (BL)	Cherry (D)	Volvo 300	Acclaim (BL)	Nova (V)	Orion (F)
Princess (BL)	Fiesta (F)	Granada (F)	Cavalier (V)	Capri (F)	Astra (V)	Sunny (D)	Sunny (D)	Orion (F)	Nova (V)
Avenger (C)	Sunny (D)	Sunny (D)	Chevette (V)	Renault 18	Mini (BL)	Granada (F)	Volvo 300	Volvo 300	Maestro (BL)

6	1977	1978	1979	1980	1981	1982	1983	1984	1985
238	120601	139204	192184	190281	159804	166942	174190	157340	157269
166	103389	114415	131667	122357	141081	135745	159119	132149	134335
107*	66088*	82638*	82938*	91661	110753	114550*	137302	125851	124143
288*	60337*	72617*	62140*	61129*	110283*	110165	127509	117442*	118817*
218*	56175*	68725	59985*	59906*	48490*	100081	119602	113071	101642
327	51763	61535*	58681	46059	36838	46412	65328*	83072*	76553
901	42816	55373	52089	41119	33631	42188*	62570	56511	73955*
476*	41128	52327	49147	39612*	32874	30412	38406*	55442	65363
702*	40934	38099	46517	31197	30854	28744	36781	51026	61358
445	35257	37928	44197	30958	28772*	28590	36753	35034	57527*
	3	3	3	3	3	2	2	2	3

Table B.5. *continued*

(c) Top ten registrations' share of the UK market and BL's share of the top ten

	1967	1968	1969	1970	1971	1972	1973	1974
Total UK new car registrations	1110266	1103862	965410	1076865	1285661	1637775	1661444	1268767
Registrations taken by top ten models	718549	737489	634987	692725	756123	950844	918854	659474
% share of total registrations taken by top ten	64.7	66.8	65.8	64.3	58.8	58.0	55.3	51.9
Registrations in top ten taken by BL	282881	297546	261574	308607	359901	357733	380914	338159
A share of total registrations taken by BL's top ten model sales	25.5	26.9	27.1	28.6	28.0	21.8	22.9	26.7
% share of top ten registrations taken by BL	39.4	40.3	41.2	44.5	47.6	37.6	41.4	51.3

Source: as Table B.1.

	1976	1977	1978	1979	1980	1981	1982	1983	1984	1985
15	1285583	1323524	1591939	1716275	1513761	1484713	1555027	1791699	1749647	1832408
94	632368	618488	722864	781145	714269	733380	803829	957561	926938	971002
	49.1	46.7	45.4	45.5	47.1	49.4	51.7	53.4	53.0	53.0
45	272791	182600	216790	205063	160647	187545	156738	241037	200514	250299
	21.2	13.8	13.6	11.9	10.6	12.6	10.1	13.4	11.5	13.7
	43.1	29.5	30.0	26.3	22.5	25.6	19.5	25.2	21.6	25.8

Table B.6. Europe's top ten models, 1984

	Austria	Belgium	Denmark	Eire	Finland	France
VW Golf/ Jetta	21467	7906	3286	2186	3552	38637
Ford Escort/ Orion	9825	7898	8389	3842	5432	57839
Fiat Uno	4626	6371	3043	1821	2883	27290
Renault R9/11	3233	10342	0	1839	0	212164
Ford Fiesta	2995	8107	3328	5224	2125	50304
Opel Kadett	12103	11781	8912	2826	3805	16615
Peugot 205	3896	6637	0	0	0	171702
Opel Ascona	9506	5283	5049	2879	3540	17821
Ford Sierra	6607	4634	8727	2359	2792	29016
Renault R5	2155	0	0	902	0	155523

Source: 'Motor Industry Survey', *Financial Times*, 11 September 1985

y	Nether-Lands	Spain	Sweden	Switzer-land	UK	W Germany	Total
00	25317	0	13895	21702	28511	313273	539332
00	30459	38470	10409	9127	208366	84164	496720
50	9754	0	1754	5162	20915	36719	451388
50	8486	77668	0	3277	27718	27962	435139
00	8109	22850	3743	0	125851	72951	349688
0	30712	0	9159	14013	56511	171718	338155
00	9840	30024	0	5574	19661	25995	303529
0	12656	0	0	9321	132149	97954	296154
0	13402	0	6738	7095	113071	88713	283154
50	6372	26062	2517	3216	15190	18342	274329

Table B.7. Production volumes of major European, American and Japanese car producers[1]

	1970	1971	1972	1973	1974	1975
British Leyland	788.7	886.7	916.2	875.8	738.5	605.1
Citroen	471.1	578.3	650.0	658.8	531.1	548.4
Peugot	525.2	559.5	603.4	684.5	596.1	563.8
Renault	1055.8	1069.2	1202.5	1293.0	1174.4	1042.3
BMW	158.6	163.8	181.9	196.1	184.7	217.5
Daimler	280.4	284.2	323.9	331.7	340.0	350.1
Volkswagen	1518.4	1622.5	1373.1	1364.1	1170.0	1050.3
Fiat	1514.4	1459.7	1481.6	1504.1	1314.0	1078.0
Honda	276.9	215.3	235.3	257.0	316.0	328.1
Mitsubishi	246.4	260.9	222.9	281.0	233.1	288.8
Nissan	899.0	1101.5	1352.2	1487.4	1255.7	1532.7
Toyota	1068.3	1400.2	1487.7	1631.9	1484.8	1714.8
Ford	2017.1	2176.3	2400.8	2495.9	2205.2	1808.0
General Motors	2979.3	4853.0	4775.3	5253.1	3585.5	3679.3

Source: as Table 3.1.

1. Production totals are of cars manufactured in the companies' domestic factories. These totals therefore exclude overseas assembly and manufacture operations.

1977	1978	1979	1980	1981	1982	1983	1984
651.1	611.6	503.8	395.8	413.4	383.1	445.4	383.3
667.3	679.0	679.3	536.4	533.9	522.3	542.5	473.8
676.1	742.3	754.5	607.0	569.3	536.5	605.6	736.6
1259.0	1240.1	1403.9	1492.3	1295.7	1491.9	1639.4	1429.1
284.8	311.8	328.3	330.1	337.8	362.6	407.5	412.4
409.1	403.7	433.2	438.8	449.0	465.5	483.4.	469.4
1277.6	1300.6	1304.5	1232.1	1150.6	1122.1	1097.8	1203.3
1130.0	1193.5	1170.1	1072.0	955.3	1071.3	1157.8	1205.3
576.6	646.8	706.4	845.5	852.2	854.4	857.7	843.8
486.4	598.3	528.6	659.6	606.9	572.6	523.7	547.8
1615.9	1620.4	1738.9	1940.6	1864.3	1815.8	1858.8	1846.4
1884.3	1982.7	2111.3	2303.3	2248.2	2258.2	2380.8	2413.1
2555.9	2557.2	2043.0	1306.9	1320.2	1104.0	1547.7	1775.3
5259.6	5284.5	5091.9	4064.5	3904.0	3173.1	3975.3	4344.6

Table B.8. Market share held by the three best-selling models from the three major UK companies

	1965	1966	1967	1968	1969	1970	1971	1972	1973
BL	23.8#	20.8#	22.3*	24.2*	24.1*	23.3*	21.8*	18.6*	16.3*
Ford	18.3#	18.6#	20.0#	22.7*	24.3*	23.9*	17.5*	22.6*	20.1*
Vauxhall	10.8#	10.1#	12.5#	12.3*	10.8*	9.4*	9.8*	8.2*	8.0*

Source: as Table B.1.

* Three models in total calculation.
#Only two models included up to 1967 so as to show market share which could then be claimed by two models.

5	1976	1977	1978	1979	1980	1981	1982	1983	1984	1985
0*	16.1*	13.8*	13.8*	11.9*	10.5*	12.2*	11.7*	13.4*	13.4*	13.8*
9*	22.4*	20.1*	20.3*	22.4*	26.8*	27.8*	26.5*	25.3*	22.7*	20.9*
3*	8.3*	8.4*	7.8*	6.0*	6.0*	6.8*	10.9*	12.0*	13.9*	14.8*

Table B.9. BL car exports to the EEC and USA, 1976–84

	1976	1977	1978	1979	1980	1981	1982	1983	1984
Belgium/Luxembourg	80121	82233	83918	53647	38265	5478	14752	7990	8785
Denmark	20212	8516	3750	1619	236	685	94	416	285
France	7836	7325	5463	6529	6435	21988	34453	34118	27518
Germany	9181	7068	9371	4530	5429	5474	2969	7535	9330
Greece	3370	378	108	13	8	5	8	4	4
Ireland	6630	7129	6093	2209	2276	2931	2696	2979	3542
Italy	17165	47063	43477	46962	54789	50002	28495	16583	14394
Netherlands	10208	8927	7209	4776	3772	5302	2269	7194	6033
Total EEC	154723	168639	159390	120285	112100	91865	85737	76819	69892
USA	75291	63428	48522	45716	25139	6264	10736	15054	1
Total	230014	232067	207912	166001	137239	98129	96473	91873	69893
Index	100	100.9	90.4	72.1	59.6	42.7	41.9	39.9	30.4

Table B.10. Change in BL exports to the EEC, 1977–84

	Increase/ decrease units	1984	1977
Belgium/Luxembourg	(73448)	8785	82233
Denmark	(8231)	285	8516
France	20193	27518	7325
W Germany	2262	9330	7068
Greece	(374)	4	378
Ireland	(3586)	3543	7129
Italy	(32669)	14394	47063
Netherlands	(2894)	6033	8927
	(98747)	69892	168639

Select Bibliography

Altshuler, A., Anderson, M., Jones, D., Roos, D. and Womack, J. (1984), *The Future of the Automobile: the Report of MIT's International Automobile Program*, London, Allen & Unwin.

Bank of England Quarterly (1981), 'Services in the UK Balance of Payments', December, pp. 519–26.

Batstone, E. (1984), *Working Order*, Oxford, Blackwell.

Bessant, J. *et al.* (1984), *The West Midlands Automobile Components Industry: Recent Changes and Future Prospects*, Birmingham, West Midlands County Council.

Bhaskar, K. (1979), *The Future of the UK Motor Industry*, London, Kogan Page.

Butler, R. D. (1981), 'Automation in the Mini Metro Manufacturing Facilities', *The Management of Automation*, August, pp. 40–54.

Central Policy Review Staff (1975), *The Future of the British Car Industry*, London, HMSO.

Centre for Policy Studies (1983), *BL: Changing Gear*, London Policy Studies Institute.

Central Statistical Office (1972). *National Income and Expenditure*, London, HMSO.

Connell, R. *et al.* (1984), *Ford of Europe, a Strategic Profile*, Harbridge House Europe (Study for Nissan).

Cutler, T., Williams, K. and Williams, J. (1986), *Keynes, Beveridge and Beyond*, London, Routledge and Kegan Paul.

Daley, A., Hitchens, D. and Wagner, K. (1985), 'Productivity, Machinery and Skills in a Sample of British and German manufacturing Plants', *National Institute Economic Review*, February, pp. 48–62.

Dept. of Employment (1970). *British Labour Statistics Yearbook*, London, HMSO.

Dept. of Trade (1979). *Overseas Trade and Statistics of the United Kingdom*, December, London, HMSO.

Edwardes, M. (1983), *Back from the Brink: An Apocalyptic Experience*, London, Collins.

Flexible Automation Systems (1984), *Opportunities and Limitations*, Bedford, IFS (Publications).

Hartley, J. (1981), *The Management of Vehicle Production*, London, Butterworth.

Hartley, J. (1985), *Robots at Work*, Bedford, IFS (Publications).

House of Commons Expenditure Committee (1974–5), *The Motor Vehicle Industry Report and Evidence*, London, HMSO.

House of Commons Expenditure Committee (1981), *Motor Industry* London, HMSO.

House of Commons Select Committee on Trade and Industry (1981), *BL plc*, London, HMSO.

House of Commons Select Committee on Trade and Industry (1982), *BL plc*, London, HMSO.

House of Commons Select Committee on Trade and Industry (1985), *BL plc*, London, HMSO.

House of Lords Select Committee on European Community (1983–4) *The Distribution, Servicing and Pricing of Motor Vehicles*, London, HMSO.

House of Lords Select Committee on Overseas Trade (1984–5), *Report and Minutes of Evidence*, London, HMSO.

Jones, D. T. (1985a), 'Vehicles' in C. Freeman, (ed.), *Technical Trends and Employment: 4. Engineering and Vehicles*, Aldershot, Gower.

Jones, D. T. (1985b), *The Import Threat to the UK Car Industry*, Brighton, Policy Research Unit.

Maxcy, G. and Silbertson, A. (1959), *The Motor Industry*, London, Allen & Unwin.

OECD (1983), *Long-term Outlook for the World Automobile Industry*, Paris, OECD.

Robson, G. (1983), *Metro*, London, Patrick Stephens.

Ryder Report (1975), *British Leyland. The Next Decade*, London, HMSO.

SMMT (1970–85), *The Motor Industry of Great Britain* (annual) London, Society of Motor Manufacturers and Traders.

Wilks, S. (1984), *Industrial Policy and the Motor Industry*, Manchester, Manchester University Press.

Williams, K., Williams, J. and Thomas, D. (1983), *Why Are the British Bad at Manufacturing?*, London, Routledge and Kegan Paul.

Williams, K. and Haslam, C. (with Williams, J. and Wardlow, A.) (1986), 'Accounting for Failure in Nationalised Industries', *Economy and Society*, vol. 15, no. 2.

Willman, P. (1984), 'The Reform of Collective Bargaining and Strike Activity at BL Cars', *Industrial Relations Journal*, vol. 15, no. 2, pp. 1–12.

Willman, P. and Winch, G. (1985), *Innovation and Management Control: Labour Relations at BL Cars*, Cambridge, Cambridge University Press.

Index

accounting procedures, 118–24
Alfa, 54, 39
Altshuler, A., 20, 50, 108
Andrews, David, 2
assembly, 5, 92, 93–4, 96, 114
  fate for AR, 54–6, 111–17
  kits, 13, 22, 84–6, 114, 115, 116
  plant, 4, 48, 56, 85
Austin, Rover, 1, 2, 4, 7, 8, 9, 10, 11, 12, 13, 19, 21, 22, 23, 24, 26, 27, 28, 30, 32, 33, 36, 38, 39, 40, 41, 44, 45, 47, 49, 50, 52, 53, 54, 55, 56, 60, 61, 63, 67, 68, 69, 70, 71, 72, 73, 74, 75, 76, 77, 79, 80, 81, 86, 89, 90, 91, 92, 93, 94, 110, 111, 112, 113, 114, 116, 118, 119, 120, 122, 123, 124, 127
Austin-Rover (inc. Austin, Morris, Triumph) models
  Allegro, 48, 69, 70, 85, 95, 96, 128, 132
  Dolomite, 70, 94, 95, 130, 132
  Herald, 132
  Land Rover, 88, 108
  Maestro, 5, 6, 7, 8, 10, 26, 37, 38, 39, 43, 46, 61, 62, 63, 70, 71, 76, 77, 79, 80, 87, 92, 93, 95, 96, 128
  MGB, 84
  Marina, 46, 69, 70, 71, 73, 74, 94, 95, 96, 130, 132
  Maxi, 43, 46, 70, 88, 94, 95, 130, 132
  Metro, 5, 6, 7, 10, 17, 19, 20, 21, 26, 27, 28, 31, 32, 36, 39, 43, 44, 45, 46, 47, 53, 55, 56, 62, 70, 71, 75, 76, 77, 78, 80, 86, 87, 88, 92, 93, 94, 95, 102, 128
  Mini, 21, 31, 39, 43, 46, 47, 48, 62, 69, 70, 75, 78, 79, 85, 87, 92, 94, 95, 96, 128, 132
  Minor, 132
  Montego, 5, 6, 7, 10, 26, 37, 38, 39, 46, 61, 62, 63, 70, 71, 72, 74, 76, 77, 78, 80, 92, 93, 95, 96, 130
  Princess, 46, 70, 94, 95, 132
  Sterling, 91
  Triumph Acclaim, 5, 22, 48, 92, 95
  TR7, 84
Austria, 136

Barr, A., 40
Barber, John, 2
Beckett, Terence, 2
Belgium, 85, 86, 136, 143
Bessant, J., 7, 28, 108
BLMC, 12, 36, 73
BMC, 1, 79, 84, 12
BMW, 38, 39, 41, 56, 58, 59, 91, 138
British Leyland, 1, 2, 3, 4, 6, 23, 30, 34, 35, 39, 41, 42, 76, 83, 88, 91, 94, 95, 96, 97, 98, 99, 100, 110, 113, 118, 119, 122, 123, 126, 134, 138, 140, 142, 143

car industry
  importance of, 107–8
  trade deficit, 105, 107–8, 109, 110, 111, 114, 116
Central Policy Review Staff (CPRS), 14, 28, 29, 32, 35, 48, 56
Chrysler, 39, 112
Citroën, 39, 138
closures, 4, 14, 17, 48, 113, 122
collective bargaining, 15, 16
competition, 12, 72–6, 98, 99, 116
  full line, 76–81, 96
components, 13, 21, 22, 28–30, 107–8
corporate organisation, 33–4
cost
  components, 28–30
  development, 51–2, 55, 71, 111
  labour, 28–31
  production, 27–32, 45–6, 47–9, 56, 63
Cutler, A., 13, 97, 104, 107, 108

Daimler Benz, 39, 138
Datsun, 84
Day, Graham, 1, 113
demand, 69, 72
  composition of, 67, 72–81, 87, 103
  level of, 67
Denmark, 86, 90, 136, 143
depreciation, 11, 49, 119, 122, 124

economics of car manufacturer, 11, 27–32, 37–40, 50–6
economies of scale, 12, 37–8, 50–4, 63
Edwardes, Sir Michael, 1, 2, 3, 4, 5, 6, 7, 9, 15, 16, 17, 18, 19, 24, 31, 33, 36, 50, 54, 60, 69, 70, 82, 85, 86, 87, 88, 89, 96, 100, 101, 118
efficiency, productive, 6, 10–12, 27
EEC, 84, 85, 89, 90, 115, 142, 143
Eire, 136
employment, 8, 13, 21, 23–8, 31, 109, 110, 111, 112, 114, 116
enterprise calculation, 3, 6, 11, 12, 87–94
Europe, 52, 84, 86, 89, 90, 91, 92, 112, 115
exchange rate, 4, 82–3, 86, 88, 89

exports, *see* markets

Fiat, 4, 39, 52, 54, 68, 86, 88, 138
  Uno, 40, 68
Finland, 136
flexibility, 51, 53, 56–66, 103
  marketing, 57–8, 60
  product-mix, 57–60, 62, 63
Ford, 28, 39, 41, 46, 51, 56, 58, 61, 62, 63, 72, 73, 76, 77, 78, 79, 88, 92, 95, 96, 109, 110, 111, 112, 114, 116, 138
  Anglia, 132
  Corsair, 132
  Cortina, 73, 74, 77, 79, 130, 132
  Escort, 40, 68, 73, 76, 77, 78, 79, 128
  Fiesta, 59, 63, 76, 77, 78, 79, 87, 88, 128, 133
  Granada, 133
  Orion, 68, 76, 77, 78, 79, 133
  Sierra, 59, 63, 73, 74, 76, 77, 78, 130
France, 68, 84, 86, 108, 109, 136, 143

Germany, West, 68, 86, 90, 91, 108, 109, 137, 143
GM, 39, 53, 71, 75, 79, 80, 88, 109, 112, 138
government
  funding, 4, 5, 17, 36, 89, 110, 111, 122–23
  policy, 13, 97–9, 109–17
Greece, 143

Harvey-Jones, J., 117
Harriman, George, 1, 25
Hattersley, Roy, 109
Hayden, George, 2, 50, 51
Heath, Edward, 8
Honda, 39, 54, 55, 62, 91, 94, 95, 110, 111, 112, 130
  Acclaim, 31, 92, 96, 128
  Ballade, 5, 22, 93
  Civic, 93
Horrocks, Ray, 2
House of Commons, 14, 26, 35, 48, 50, 60, 88, 108, 119
  of Lords, 82, 99, 104, 117

imports, 13, 73, 76–8, 107, 110, 115, 116
industrial relations, *see* work practices
inflation, 4, 98, 99
interest charges, 11, 49, 119, 123–4
investment, 5, 6, 7, 12, 14, 18, 21, 22, 90, 102, 114
  strategy, 35–8, 40–66
Italy, 68, 84, 85, 86, 90, 108, 109, 137, 143
Ireland, 143
Isuzu, 39

Jaguar, 2, 41, 60, 83, 84, 127
Japan, 28, 85, 93, 108, 109, 115
Jones, Daniel, 7, 38, 50, 85, 107, 110, 114

labour relations, *see* work practices
Lord, Len, 1, 25
losses, *see* profits

manufacturing
  British, 13, 82–3, 97–9, 100–2, 107–8
  flexible, *see* flexibility
  trade, 99, 103–6, 116–17
market
  classes, 5, 12
  exports, 5, 8, 9, 12, 13, 68–9, 81–4, 107
  fleet, 73–4
  limitations, 12–13, 26, 33, 49, 62, 67–96, 102–3, 111, 113
  safeguarding, 13, 97, 105, 114–17
  share, 5, 6, 7, 9, 10, 12, 68–70, 72, 74, 76, 77–81, 94–6, 104, 116
Mazda, 39
Mercedes, 39, 56, 91, 92
MIT International Automobile Program, 50, 108
Mitsubishi, 39, 54, 138
model
  name, *see* appropriate manufacturer
  new, 5, 6, 7, 8, 11
  quality, 70–2, 87–8
  range, 5, 10, 39, 48, 58, 67, 69–71, 94–6
Morris, 1, 2, 10, 21, 23, 24, 26, 72, 81, 83, 84, 94, 127
Musgrove, Harold, 19, 20, 43, 72

Netherlands, 137, 143
Nissan, 39, 58, 59, 71, 72, 76, 138
  Blue Bird, 59
  Cherry, 59, 133
  Laurel, 59
  Micra, 58, 59
  Prairie, 59
  Sylvia, 59
  Sunny, 58, 59, 133

output, 4, 7, 8, 9, 10, 23–7, 31, 38–44, 49, 55, 93, 110
over-capacity, 3, 27, 42–4, 48–50, 62, 63, 68, 102, 108, 114
  manning, 3, 101

Park, Alex, 2
Peugeot, 54, 112, 114, 138, 139, 140
plants
  Canley, 42, 81
  Cofton Hackett, 43
  Coventry, 48
  Cowley, 1, 4, 5, 38, 42, 48, 49, 60, 61, 62, 63, 93, 114
  Dagenham, 58, 59, 61, 62, 114

Halewood, 114
Longbridge, 1, 4, 5, 7, 8, 17, 19, 21, 36, 38, 42, 43, 45, 46, 48, 49, 60, 61, 62, 63, 86, 93, 102, 114
peripheral, 4, 25, 42, 48, 81, 124
Seneffe, 48, 85
Solihull, 42, 48, 81
Speke, 42, 48, 81
Swindon, 1
Wolfsburg, 58
policy, *see* government
Porsche, 51, 91
pound, *see* exchange rate
Prime Minister, 4, 98
processes
body in white, 19, 20, 21, 32, 47, 61
final assembly, 19, 20, 21, 32, 36, 43, 45, 51
paint, 19, 20, 36, 43
power-train, 21, 32
productivity
labour, 7, 10, 13, 14–27, 35, 67, 98
capital, 10–11, 27, 33, 35, 40–56
product-led recovery, 5, 9, 70, 98
profits, 2, 3, 6, 8, 11, 49, 63, 108, 118, 119–24
and losses, 2, 3, 11, 118, 119–24

redundancy, 6, 10, 14, 17, 25–7, 31–2, 113
reorganization, 1, 11, 41, 119
Renault, 4, 11, 39, 40, 54, 68, 76, 88, 116, 138
Robinson, Derek, 17
robots, 10, 37, 44–5, 51–2, 58, 59–62, 109
Rover, 5, 39, 42, 43, 48, 62, 82, 83, 92, 95, 96, 97, 98, 100, 101, 102, 103, 105, 109, 132
Ryder, Sir Don, 2, 3, 4, 6, 34, 84

Saab, 39, 53, 54
sales, 7, 8, 9, 10, 67, 68–70, 81, 87–8, 91
shipbuilding, 113
shop stewards, 6, 15, 16
Spain, 85, 137
stocks, 10, 26
Stokes, Lord, 2
strategy, 3, 4, 5, 6, 7, 11, 12, 13, 16, 24, 33, 48, 60, 85–92, 100–2
strikes, 15–16, 17–18, 26, 33
Suzuki, 39
Sweden, 109, 137
Switzerland, 137

Talbot, 56
technology
automation, 5, 36–8, 43
flexibility of, *see* flexibility
justification of, 44–50, 56
limitations of, 50–6
methods of, 59–63
new, 4, 5, 6, 7, 8, 10, 11, 12, 13, 14, 15, 16, 18, 20, 24, 25, 26, 32, 89
Thatcher, Margaret, 98, 100
trade unions, 6, 15, 16, 17, 98, 99
Toyota, 39, 138
Triumph, 2, 41, 48, 81, 82, 83

USA, 55, 91, 108, 109, 142

Vauxhall, 28, 56, 72, 73, 74, 75, 76, 78, 79, 87, 95, 110, 112, 114, 140
Astra, 40, 76, 77, 79, 80
Cavalier, 40, 74, 76, 77, 78, 79 80, 87, 130
Chevette, 128, 133
Nova, 76, 77, 78, 79, 80, 128
Viva, 128, 132
value added, 13, 109, 110, 111, 112, 114–16
Volvo, 38, 39, 54, 71, 76, 92, 96, 133
VW, 4, 22, 37, 39, 40, 56, 59, 68, 71, 76, 87, 88, 116, 138
Audi, 58, 59, 91
Golf, 40
Jetta, 58
Passat, 59
Polo, 59, 87, 88, 96
Scirrocco, 58, 59

Walters, Sir Alan, 98
Weinstock, Lord, 117
Whittaker, Derek, 2
Willman, P., 7, 8, 15, 16, 17, 19, 20, 27, 43, 45, 46, 47, 55, 63, 70, 88
work practices, 6, 7, 10, 11, 12, 14–21, 24–7, 30–3, 35, 36, 44, 47, 49, 89, 98, 101

About the Authors

Karel and John Williams teach economic history at University College of Wales, Aberystwyth. They are joint authors of *Why are the British Bad at Manufacturing?* (with D. Thomas, 1983) and *Keynes, Beveridge and Beyond* (with T. Cutler, 1986). Colin Haslam teaches economics at North East London Polytechnic. He has worked with Karel and John Williams on various projects, including *The Aberystwyth Report on Coal* (1985).

The Breakdown of Austin Rover

A Case-Study in the Failure of Business Strategy
and Industrial Policy